Bangladesh National Nutrition Services

A WORLD BANK STUDY

Bangladesh National Nutrition Services

Assessment of Implementation Status

Kuntal K. Saha, Masum Billah, Purnima Menon, Shams El Arifeen, and Nkosinathi V. N. Mbuya

WORLD BANK GROUP

Contents

Boxes

Figures

Tables

Acknowledgments

This study was conducted by a team comprising Kuntal Saha, Ashfaqul Chowdhury, Muhammad Bhuiyan, Shuchita Rahman, Tahsin Rahman, Waziha Rahman, Md. Redoy (International Food Policy Research Institute), Purnima Menon (International Food Policy Research Institute, with support from Transform Nutrition), Masum Billah and Abdulllah Khan (International Centre for Diarrhoeal Disease Research, Bangladesh), Shams El Arifeen (International Centre for Diarrhoeal Disease Research, Bangladesh; with support from Transform Nutrition), Peter Davis (consultant), and Nazneen Akhtar (consultant). Appreciated contributions to the planning of this study and review of the preliminary report were given by Chris Buckley, Melkamnesh Alemu, Shehlina Ahmed (Department for International Development–Bangladesh), Meaghan Byers, Sylvia Islam (Canadian International Development Agency), Shannon Young, Miranda Beckman (United States Agency for International Development–Bangladesh), Iffat Mahmud (operations officer, Health, Nutrition, and Population Global Practice), and the staff of National Nutrition Services/Institute for Public Health and Nutrition. The World Bank task team leader for this study was Nkosinathi Mbuya (senior nutrition specialist, Health, Nutrition, and Population Global Practice).

The report was peer reviewed by Lalita Bhattacharjee (nutritionist, Food and Agriculture Organization of the United Nations–Bangladesh), Claudia Rokx (lead health specialist, Health, Nutrition, and Population Global Practice), and Dinesh Nair (senior health specialist, Health, Nutrition, and Population Global Practice). Alicia Hetzner edited the report.

Executive Summary

In 2009, the Annual Program Review of the Health, Nutrition, and Population Sector Program (HNPSP) of the World Bank recommended scaling up nutrition interventions in Bangladesh through mainstreaming critical nutrition interventions in the services provided through the country's Director General of Health Services (DGHS) and Director General of Family Planning (DGFP). To achieve this goal, the country made nutrition a priority. The National Nutrition Services (NNS) has been pursuing a variety of key strategies and actions. In 2011, the operational plan (OP) of NNS was approved by the government of Bangladesh. According to the OP, the mainstreamed NNS interventions should be implemented through the existing health system from July 2011 to June 2016.

The overall objective of this study is to assess the effectiveness of the delivery of the different components of NNS and to assess whether the various interventions are being delivered to the intended beneficiaries at an adequate quality and coverage. The study's specific objectives are to do the following:

1. Systematically assess the implementation of NNS to identify the achievements, determine the bottlenecks that adversely impact these achievements, and highlight potential solutions to ensure smooth delivery of the program.
2. Assess the quality and coverage of the delivery of the implemented interventions as a mainstreamed delivery approach.
3. Make recommendations to further strengthen the implementation of a mainstreamed nutrition-service delivery approach in Bangladesh.

Research Approach and Methods

To assess the implementation processes and the quality of NNS, detailed research questions were formulated under five major domains: (1) management and support services, (2) training and capacity development, (3) service delivery, (4) monitoring and evaluation, and (5) exposure to interventions. The specific research questions were defined to address the overarching objectives of NNS and the pathways through which NNS interventions could achieve their expected impacts.

The study used a mixed methods approach. For example, it combined document review with in-depth interviews of the key informants: NNS core team members and other key stakeholders at the national level; and managers and service providers of NNS interventions at district, *upazila*, and community levels in four selected districts. In addition, focus group discussions were conducted with NNS providers and beneficiaries or potential beneficiaries at the community level. Survey data were collected in six selected districts. These data were acquired through a facility survey, a health care provider survey, observation of the service delivery for antenatal care, management of children younger than five years of age, and exit interviews.

Results

Design: Intervention and Delivery Platform Choices

Two central issues related to the design of NNS program emerged from this research. The first issue is the lack of specificity in choosing the number of interventions, which has led to too many interventions being coordinated and delivered by NNS.

The second issue is the choice of delivery platforms to reach scale for the different interventions. The current choice of platforms relies primarily on public health curative care facilities. It invests in only a limited manner in the preventive outreach platforms. These curative platforms are not designed to close the gaps among the essential nutrition interventions.

The research highlighted that there were too many intervention area components in the original OP for NNS to deal effectively with in the required timespan. The NNS might have been more successful at ensuring effective implementation with a narrower focus on a limited number of intervention areas. Examples are infant and young child feeding (IYCF), micronutrients, severe acute malnutrition (SAM)/community-based management of acute malnutrition (CMAM) and nutrition during antenatal care (ANC)/pregnancy for service delivery.

Governance and Institutional Arrangements

The study's results indicate that the maintenance of strong and stable leadership of NNS is an essential element to ensure integrated and well-coordinated comprehensive service delivery for the agency. The current arrangement is unable to ensure effective implementation and coordination of NNS. The reasons are recruitment and retention challenges for the Directorship of the Institute for Public Health and Nutrition (IPHN) and its failure to ensure effective coordination vis-à-vis the other line directors within the Health Ministry. For effective coordination, a mechanism that ranks above the Line Directorates that have to deliver services is important. Establishing such an overarching mechanism is a fundamental and serious challenge for an institution such as NNS. The current arrangement could be strengthened to provide technical inputs and function as an executive secretariat for nutrition within the health system. However, the current arrangement does not have adequate convening or coordinating power as a result of NNS's having been positioned at the same level as the other Line Directorates.

There are additional significant capacity and workload-related challenges within NNS/IPHN that hamper effective implementation of NNS. Among the areas of concern identified were NNS's capacity to (1) develop feasible and specific implementation plans for intervention delivery, (2) develop careful training approaches that work, (3) manage records on the training roll-out, and (4) manage NNS's large budgets. Development partners certainly could support some of these capacity challenges. However, it is not clear that NNS has developed a clear "drawdown" strategy for development partner support to NNS.

Training and Roll-Out

The operational assessment and interviews at the national level indicate that NNS training is getting underway after delays in the first year. However, record keeping of the training is inadequate. This reality makes it difficult to assess exactly which types of training and support activities were completed in each upazila and how many people at which level were trained. Ensuring systematic record keeping and consolidation of information around training likely also could address some of the training audit issues raised by interviewees.

From a training design perspective, materials that were reviewed by the research team indicated that training manuals were dense but contained limited instructions for facilitators. If NNS intervention package is streamlined and prioritized, the training manuals could be revised accordingly. The training manuals are being revised. However, to the research team's knowledge, there is no documented structured identification of nutritional capacity gaps and assessment of training needs and effectiveness.

Other training challenges are that a large number of frontline health staff receive training for a variety of other governmental and NGO programs. Combining trainings makes the identification and branding of NNS training quite difficult. Thus, monitoring sources of training and the extent of workers' training are very challenging. Nevertheless, monitoring is essential to ensure efficiencies in training on similar topics for health professionals in an integrated health system.

Finally, several ongoing problems concern logistics and supplies for nutrition-related services. For example, upazila staff received nutrition training. However, they did not receive logistical support. They received nonfunctioning equipment, and they experienced a long lag time between submitting requests for logistics and receiving them. NNS now has initiated procurement of logistics through the Central Medical Stores Depot. Continued work by NNS is needed to streamline procurement with the depot.

Service Delivery

Service delivery under NNS is intended to occur through diverse delivery platforms. They included Integrated Management of Childhood Illnesses (IMCI)+Nutrition Corners, ANC, inpatient care, sick-child visits at community clinics, and outreach through health assistants (HAs) and family welfare volunteers (FWVs).

- *IMCI+Nutrition Corners.* IMCI protocols already include guidance on specific nutrition-related activities (such as checking on feeding, assessing weights). However, this component is lagging behind the basic clinical diagnostic and prescriptive nature of sick-child care. Emphasizing the nutrition activities as part of ongoing IMCI training can strengthen this activity.

    However, quantitative data indicate that the average time each patient receives from a health care provider is approximately 3.5 minutes. Children coming to IMCI+Nutrition Corners are primarily sick children. Therefore, targeting delivery of infant and young child feeding (IYCF) counselling to take place during a short illness-focused contact is fundamentally challenging (wrong age group, sick children only).

- *ANC.* ANC protocols also include some nutrition focus, and providers do include several nutrition-specific actions in the ANC provision. The ANC platform is fundamentally a preventive focused platform. It directly reaches the targets for the nutrition interventions, that is, pregnant women—but only those who are seeking these services, an estimated 25 percent of all pregnant women.

- *Referral and inpatient care for SAM.* According to the health facility assessment carried out by the research team, referrals for severe acute malnutrition (SAM) are limited or inaccurate because providers are not investing in weighing and measuring the children who come to the IMCI+Nutrition Corners. In most facilities surveyed, the service utilization data show the number of SAM children managed in the previous months was usually two or fewer. SAM cases need careful investigation. Referrals also should be followed up and appropriate treatment given to comply with national guidelines.

- *Sick-child visits at community clinics.* Case observations of illness management of children younger than five years of age reveals extremely poor performance related to weighing sick children seen in the community clinics, in spite of a greater availability of equipment than in IMCI+Nutrition Corners. Strengthening care protocols for sick children brought to the community clinics, and ensuring logistics supply and monitoring and supervision of SAM/MAM (management of severe malnutrition) screening also could strengthen nutrition-focused service components.

- *Outreach through HAs/FWVs.* The team did not examine service delivery by HAs and FWVs because it was beyond the scope of the survey. Qualitative interviews with these frontline staff revealed their almost complete lack of awareness or knowledge about nutrition-related services and low exposure to NNS training. A detailed assessment of training processes that relate to these frontline workers is essential, as is an assessment of what specific roles they are to play within NNS.

Overall, there is great variability in the integration of nutrition interventions and actions into these delivery platforms. Much remains to be done to truly integrate nutrition into these health services. Some areas of better performance do exist, such as IMCI+Nutrition and ANC. However, deep challenges relating to service delivery and supervision exist for the community clinics and the outreach services by the HAs and FWAs. Training coverage among these service providers also are low. To the research team's knowledge, there was no piloting of specific NNS interventions within each of these platforms before these services were mainstreamed on a larger scale. Appropriate piloting would have revealed some of these problems regarding workload and choice of platforms. There also is no ongoing learning or review process in place to assess implementation challenges.

Monitoring

Overall findings on monitoring to strengthen NNS performance are that several challenges determine whether program performance is on track. First, record keeping for monitoring purposes within NNS system appears weak. Information on implementation roll-out and development partner support to geographic and technical areas also was hard to get or was unavailable.

Second, a set of nutrition indicators has been developed to mainstream into the health management information system (HMIS). Nonetheless, there are challenges with some indicators. For example, early initiation of breastfeeding, low birth weight, and stunting are population-level indicators that are close to impossible to assess in a facility-based HMIS. In addition, there is a legitimate concern about overloading frontline workers with excessive record keeping.

Third, a system for technical monitoring by experts of service quality is largely absent. NNS staff at the Dhaka level are too busy and do not appear to make the field visits to examine program performance.

Recommendations

Design-Related Recommendations

- An expert committee, potentially a Steering Committee for Nutrition Implementation, would prioritize and choose several key services to deliver as part of NNS. The committee would test the feasibility of these services with the different Director General of Health Services (DGHS) delivery platforms for practicality of delivery and potential for population coverage and impact.
- The Ministry of Health and Family Welfare (MoHFW) would redevelop very specific implementation plans that map direct nutrition interventions (DNIs) to specific delivery platforms and help identify the platforms best able to reach maximum coverage for specific DNIs.
- MoHFW would explore the use of other platforms, including those of nongovernmental organizations (NGO), to extend their reach and achieve

greater coverage. A few NGOs in Bangladesh have community-level health care providers who can supplement NNS workers.

Institutional/Governance-Related Recommendations

- MoHFW would elevate all nutrition/NNS coordination activities to be within the DGHS leadership to ensure effective coordination.
- MoHFW would draw on development partners and technical institutes/actors in a careful, strategic manner for specific planning, capacity building, and technical support activities. A comprehensive document that maps the role of each development partner is needed so that the support can be utilized optimally.
- MoHFW would establish clear tasks for key development partners and funders to support NNS.

Training-Related Recommendations

- In the immediate short term, NNS would ensure excellent and transparent (ideally web-based) record keeping, external monitoring, and consolidation of information on training activities. These steps, in particular, could address some of the training audit issues raised by interviewees.
- NNS would draw on development partners and strong implementing organizations to develop a very detailed implementation roll-out plan that is feasible and in line with goals for coverage and impact.
- NNS would invest in establishing a high quality training unit, in partnership with strong technical partners.

Service Delivery-Related Recommendations

- NNS would consider integrating feasibility assessments, technical review missions, and other learning approaches to assess the delivery of at least a few prioritized critical interventions.
- NNS would explore the use of the community groups and community support groups attached to each community clinic to raise awareness of, and demand for, better nutrition-related services.
- MoHFW would move away from IMCI+Nutrition Corners as the central NNS delivery platform. Invest more heavily in an alternative, predominantly outreach-based platform to deliver core preventive NNS services to households and children, such as well-child clinics at all existing health facilities at upazila levels and below. In parallel, ensure that overall IMCI service delivery remains a focus for sick-child care.
- MoHFW would reexamine and clarify the role of HAs and FWAs, building capacity (through training) and monitoring/incentivization for them to deliver preventive nutrition services.

Monitoring-Related Recommendations

- NNS would strengthen its record keeping, and reporting is a key focus at this stage of program implementation.
- First, NNS needs to make a careful review of the current set of NNS indicators for inclusion in the Reproductive Health Management Information System. Second, rather than the nutrition outcomes, such as low birth weight or stunting, what should be prioritized are a few indicators that indicate extent and quality of service delivery.
- A system for technical monitoring by experts of service quality is a critical need. NNS should draw on the capacity of development partners to help develop a streamlined quality assurance system. It could include a web-based data input system for recording site visits and for helping facilitate organized and systematic field supervision visits.

Conclusions

This assessment of the current state of NNS is drawn from multiple-data sources. It is meant primarily to inform revisions to NNS approach and to refocus and identify critical areas for continued investment and support. Although the assessment has identified several substantial challenges to NNS, the overall NNS effort is an ambitious, but valuable, approach to examine how best to support nutrition actions through an existing health system with diverse platforms.

Focusing, first, on some of the critical challenges related to leadership and coordination, and, second, on embedding a small core set of interventions into well-matched[1] health system delivery platforms is most likely to help achieve scale and impact. Strategic investments in ensuring transparency, engaging available technical partners for monitoring and implementation support, and not shying away from other potential high coverage outreach platforms, such as some NGO platforms, also could prove fruitful. The Government of Bangladesh, and the health system in particular, must lead the effort to deliver nutrition. Nonetheless, it is clear that development partners who have expressed a commitment to nutrition must coordinate their own activities both among themselves and with the government and provide the support that can deliver nutrition's potential for Bangladesh.

Note

1. For scale, target populations, and potential for impact.

Abbreviations

AFWO	assistant family welfare officer
AHI	assistant health inspector
ANC	antenatal care
BCC	behavior change communication
BDT	*Bangladeshi taka*
BINP	Bangladesh Integrated Nutrition Project/Programme
CHCP	community health care provider
CHW	community health worker
CIDA	Canadian International Development Agency
CMAM	community-based management of acute malnutrition
CMSD	central medical stores depot
DFID	Department for International Development (UK)
DGFP	Director General of Family Planning
DGHS	Director General of Health Services
DNI	direct nutrition intervention
DPM	deputy program manager
DS	district superintendent
ECD	early childhood development
EPI	Expanded Program of Immunization
FAO	Food and Agriculture Organization of the United Nations
FPA	family planning assistant
FWA	family welfare assistant
FWC	family welfare clinic
FWV	family welfare volunteer
GAVI	Global Alliance for Vaccines and Immunizations
GHNDR	Global Practice Health and Nutrition, Director's Office
GMP	growth monitoring and promotion
GoB	Government of Bangladesh
HA	health assistant

HI	health inspector
HKI	Helen Keller International
HMIS	Health Management Information System
HNP	health, nutrition, and population
HNPSP	Health, Nutrition, and Population Sector Program
HPNSDP	Health, Population, and Nutrition Sector Development Program
HSDP	Health Sector Development Program
ICDDR,B	International Centre for Diarrhoeal Disease Research, Bangladesh
IDD	iodine deficiency disorder
IFA	iron-folic acid
IFPRI	International Food Policy Research Institute
IMCI	Integrated Management of Childhood Illnesses
IMCI+N	IMCI and Nutrition Corners
INGO	international nongovernmental organization
IPHN	Institute for Public Health and Nutrition
IRB	institutional review board
IYCF	infant and young child feeding
LBW	low birth weight
M&E	monitoring and evaluation
MAM	management of acute malnutrition
MDGs	Millennium Development Goals
NGO	nongovernmental organization
MNP	micronutrient powder
MNS	micronutrient supplements
MO	medical officer
MUAC	mid-upper arm circumference
NCD	noncommunicable disease
NNP	National Nutrition Program
NNS	National Nutrition Services
OP	operational plan (GoB)
ORS	oral rehydration solution
PM	program manager
PNC	postnatal care
RHMIS	Routine Health Management Information Systems
SACMO	subassistant community medical officer
SAM	severe acute malnutrition
SPRING	Strengthening Partnerships, Results and Innovations for Nutrition Globally

ToT	training of trainers
UFPO	upazila family planning officer
UHC	upazila health complex
UHFPO	upazila health and family planning officer
UHFWC	upazila health and family welfare centre
UNDAP	United Nations Development Assistance Plan
UNICEF	United Nations Children's Fund
USAID	United States Agency for International Development

CHAPTER 1

Introduction

Background

Overall, Bangladesh has made laudable progress on many aspects of human development. This progress should ensure continued and sustained improvements in economic growth and social mobility. The country also is on track to achieve certain of the global targets of the Millennium Development Goals (MDGs) related to health, nutrition, and population (HNP). These targets include child mortality and combating human immunodeficiency virus (HIV)/ acquired immune deficiency syndrome (AIDS), in both of which Bangladesh has outperformed other countries in the region.

However, all of these improvements have not translated into positive effects on maternal and child nutrition. Stunting rates for children 0–60 months are an indicator of chronic malnutrition and are associated with cognitive development, productivity, and earning potential in adult life. In Bangladesh, from 2004 to 2007, stunting rates declined by 8 percent from 51 percent to 43 percent, respectively. Between 2007 and 2011, these indicators have almost stagnated (Bangladesh Demographic and Health Survey 2011), the prevalence of stunting declined by just 2 percent to 41 percent. The prevalence of underweight, the indicator used for the second target of the first MDG (1C), declined from 43 percent in 2004 to 41 percent in 2007 to 36 percent in 2011.

This situation is of grave concern, given that malnutrition between conception and 24 months of age can cause irreversible damage to health, growth, and cognitive development. Malnutrition leads to higher child morbidity and mortality, lower IQ, lower school achievement, reduced adult productivity, and lower earnings. The fallout from this malnutrition could result in a future significant reduction in gross domestic product of 2 percent–3 percent per year.

For several decades, the Ministry of Health and Family Welfare (MoHFW) of the Government of Bangladesh has recognized the need for large-scale intervention to prevent and control malnutrition among large segments of the population. With the assistance of development partners, MoHFW has made substantial investments to address malnutrition. The country's first major nutrition program was the Bangladesh Integrated Nutrition Program (BINP), implemented from 1996 to 2002. The core component of BINP was the community-based nutrition activities implemented by NGOs. The project covered 61 upazila and reached approximately 16 percent of the rural population. BINP ended in 2002. The same activities were continued under the National Nutrition Program (NNP) from 2006 to 2011.

The NNP formulation was based on the BINP and was designed to cover approximately 25 percent of the population. In 2004, this program was implemented in almost twice as many (109) upazila, including BINP upazila, and was integrated into the Health, Nutrition and Population Sector Program (HNPSP) as the NNP. In 2010, NNP was expanded to 172 upazila. It ended in May 2011 in alignment with the completion of the Health, Nutrition and Population Sector Program (HNPSP).

The design of the NNP included a core package of area-based community nutrition services. They included behavior change communication (BCC) at community and household levels to address maternal, infant, child, and adolescent feeding and care practices that affect nutrition; growth monitoring and promotion; micronutrient supplementation (MNS; vitamin A for children 9–59 months and iron-folate for pregnant women); biannual deworming of severely malnourished children (12–59 months) and adolescents (13–19 years); utilization of nutrition, health, and food security services; food supplementation (*pushti* packets) for severely malnourished children younger than two years of age; and gardening and poultry activities to improve food security. (The gardening and poultry activities were discontinued in 2006.)

NNP services were provided through community nutrition centers, each covering a population of approximately 1,200. Nongovernmental organizations (NGOs) were contracted to deliver services through 36,764 community nutrition centers in 172 upazila in 46 districts, with considerable variation in the number of community nutrition centers managed by each NGO. Community nutrition promoters, or *Pushti apa*, directly provide the services from a community nutrition center. Their activities are supervised by community nutrition officers, who, in turn, are supervised by field supervisors.

Under HNPSP, nutrition activities were the purview of two separate operational plans (OPs): the NNP-OP and the MNS OP. A limited set of nutrition activities was delivered through health facilities under the MNS OP. Community-based nutrition services were undertaken through NNP-OP. However, there was a recognized lack of coordination as well as duplication of activities between these two OPs. Moreover, the NNP interventions were being delivered by contracted NGOs that had fragile or no links with the mainstream health system.

Additional nutrition activities were being implemented by various ministries/divisions and development partners, but these activities were neither well coordinated nor adequately monitored. The cost of NNP was another concern for MoHFW. The total estimated cost of the NNP-OP (FY2003–11) was Tk. 1,251 crore. However, it was implemented in phases in approximately 173 upazila that covered only 34 percent of the entire population.

In this regard, the Annual Program Review of HNPSP in 2009 recommended that, to accelerate progress in reducing the persistently high rates of maternal and child malnutrition, in June 2011, the Government of Bangladesh commit to mainstream and scale-up the delivery of essential nutrition interventions into health (Directorate General of Health Services [DGHS]) and family planning services (Directorate General of Family Planning [DGFP]) through the HNP sectorwide program—Health, Population and Nutrition Sector Development Program (HPNSDP, 2011–2016).

The main goal of HNPSDP is to improve priority health, nutrition, and population services to accelerate the achievement of HNP-related MDGs (GoB 2011c). These priority services include interventions to improve the nutritional status, especially of pregnant women and children less than five years of age. The government made a decision to accelerate the progress of reducing highly prevalent undernutrition among mothers and children by (1) mainstreaming the implementation of nutrition interventions into health and family planning services through DGHS and DGFP services; (2) scaling up the provision of area-based community nutrition; and (3) updating the National Plan of Action on Nutrition in the light of recent food and nutrition policies, among other priority actions (GoB 2011b).

To achieve this goal, nutrition has been made a priority for the proposed sector program and a variety of key strategies and actions are being pursued. These include Growth Monitoring and Promotion (GMP), behavior change communications (BCC) to improve good nutritional practices, vitamin A supplementation, zinc supplementation during treatment of diarrhea, iron-folic acid supplementation for pregnant women, iron supplementation and deworming for adolescent girls, treatment of moderate and severe acute malnutrition (SAM), training and capacity building, and coordination of nutrition activities across different sectors (GoB 2011b).

In addition, the mainstreamed program is guided by two main principles:

1. The program focuses on the activities within its mandate and for which it has the capacity as well as the comparative advantage to act. For the key activities that lie outside the mandate of the health sector, National Nutrition Service (NNS) plays a coordination as well as an advocacy role. NNS ensures active engagement with other key sectors (for example, ministries of agriculture, food, and industry).
2. The nutrition program seeks to intervene at the different stages using a life-cycle approach—pregnancy, delivery/neonatal, postpartum, postnatal, childhood, adolescents, newlyweds—but with a strong focus on the "window of opportunity," that is, pregnancy through the first two years of life (1,000 days).

Before 2009, NGOs were contracted out for area-based community nutrition activities under the previous health sector program, HNPSP. In 2009, the Annual Program Review of HNPSP recommended that, to scale up the nutrition interventions in the country, the only option would be to mainstream the critical nutrition interventions via the services provided through the DGHS and DGFP.

To mainstream these interventions, HPNSDP has made nutrition a priority. In addition, NNS is pursuing a variety of key strategies and actions. In 2011, NNS-OP was approved by the Executive Committee of the National Economic Council in the HPNSDP Steering Committee meeting. According to the OP, the mainstreamed NNS interventions should be implemented through the existing DGHS and DGFP from July 2011 to June 2016.

Two years after the approval of NNS-OP, the World Bank commissioned an operations research study to understand the status of NNS implementation and progress.

Objectives of Operations Research

The overall stated objectives of this study were to gather information on the effectiveness of the delivery of the different components of national nutrition service (NNS) and to assess whether these interventions are being delivered to the intended beneficiaries at adequate quality and coverage. The specific objectives of this study were to do the following:

1. Systematically assess the *implementation of NNS* to identify what results (inputs and outputs) have been achieved and where the bottlenecks or constraints are that hamper achievements and to highlight potential solutions to ensure smooth delivery of the program.
2. Assess the *quality and coverage of the delivery* of the implemented interventions in relation to using a mainstreamed delivery approach.
3. *Identify clear lessons* (including prerequisites) *and make recommendations* on how to strengthen the implementation of a mainstreamed nutrition-service-delivery approach in Bangladesh.

Results from this operations research study will be useful in assessing the quality and coverage of the mainstreamed delivery. The study will help to provide recommendations on how to strengthen the implementation process of NNS delivery in Bangladesh.

Methods

This operations research was conducted using mixed methods—both qualitative and quantitative approaches were used to gather data on the overarching objectives of the study. For the qualitative research component, in-depth interviews of the key informants, such as National Nutrition Service (NNS) core team members and other key stakeholders at the national level, managers and service providers of NNS interventions at district, upazila, and community levels, were conducted. In addition, focus group discussions were conducted with NNS providers and beneficiaries or potential beneficiaries at the community level. For the quantitative research component, data collection included facility assessments, surveys of current service providers, observation of service delivery at antenatal care and management of children younger than five years of age, and exit interviews with clients. Given the limited roll-out of NNSand the budget available for this study, a household survey to examine population-level use of NNS and contact with NNS workers was not conducted.

Major Domains of Research, Specific Research Questions, and Data Sources

Given the primary objectives of this study—to assess the implementation processes of NNS and to assess the quality of NNS—detailed research questions have been formulated that span five major domains of implementation. These domains include the following:

1. Management and support services
2. Training and capacity development
3. Service delivery
4. Monitoring and evaluation mechanisms
5. Exposure to interventions by potential users.

In table 1.1, the specific research questions under each domain have been laid out for each of the eight major components of NNS and are aligned with the key

Table 1.1 Major Domains, Related Specific Research Questions, and Planned Data Collection

Major domains	Specific research questions	Data sources to address research questions
1. Management and Support Services	a. Do implementation plans exist for the different interventions?	• Content review of NNS operational documents
	b. What are the overall institutional arrangements for delivery of NNS interventions through the health system?	• National-level in-depth interviews with NNS staff and other stakeholders in the health system
	c. How do NNS staff engage with and support planned NNS activities to enable delivery on nutrition results?	• National-level in-depth interviews with other nutrition stakeholders
	d. Did the supervision and management occur as planned? What is the extent of intended supervision and management activities?	
2. Training and Capacity Development	a. What are the institutional arrangements for *training* for each NNS intervention?	• Content review of NNS operational documents
	b. To what extent have training and performance improvement measures been rolled out for all NNS interventions?	• National-level in-depth interviews with NNS staff and other stakeholders in the health system
	c. To what extent have NNS staff and implementing staff from the health system been exposed to NNS training and performance improvement inputs?	• National-level in-depth interviews with other nutrition stakeholders
	d. Did the training occur as intended and to what extent? What are the participation and engagement of trainers and recipients in the training?	• Service provider surveys

table continues next page

Table 1.1   Major Domains, Related Specific Research Questions, and Planned Data Collection *(continued)*

Major domains	*Specific research questions*	*Data sources to address research questions*
3. Delivery of Services	• What is the overall *fidelity* to planned implementation and *quality* of service delivery of each NNS intervention by health workers at different levels? Specifically: i. Is promotion of good nutritional practices through nutrition education happening during facility-based service contacts (MO/SACMO/MA/Nurses/FWV) and during community-based nutrition activities? ii. Are regular weight and height measurements of children 0–59 months happening during facility-based service contacts (MO/SACMO/MA/Nurses/FWV) and during community-based nutrition activities (FWA, HA, CHCP)? iii. Do service providers know how to utilize the information they gain from Growth Monitoring and Promotion (GMP) to address the specific issues an individual child is facing? iv. Is distribution of micronutrients to different target groups in place at different levels of the service delivery system? v. To what extent do the diagnosis and treatment of SAM/MAM by the service providers follow guidelines at all facilities and at the community level? Is a structured referral system working?	• Service provider surveys • Facility assessments (record review) • Structured observations • Focus group discussions with service providers • In-depth interviews with service providers
4. Monitoring and Evaluation	• What are the current arrangements for M&E of NNS interventions? How well is NNS monitoring integrated with the broader health system monitoring? For example: i. Are nutrition indicators included in the current HMIS? Which ones? Do they cover all key NNS interventions? ii. What are the available mechanisms to collect routine information on nutrition service contacts and anthropometric measurements?	• National-level in-depth interviews with NNS staff • Service provider surveys • Facility assessments (record review) • Focus group discussions with service providers • In-depth interviews with service providers
5. Exposure to Interventions	• What is the level of exposure to different NNS delivery components among household members who are potential users of NNS?	• Exit interviews and/or • User surveys with recently delivered women and households with children younger than 5 years of age

Note: CHCP = community health care provider; FWA = family welfare assistant; FWV = family welfare volunteer; HA = health assistant; HMIS = health management information system; MA; MAM = management of acute malnutrition; M&E = monitoring and evaluation; MO = medical officer; NNS = National Nutrition Services; SACMO = subassistant community medical officer; SAM = severe acute malnutrition.

research questions in each of the five domains. These research questions have been defined to address the overarching objectives of NNS and the pathways through which NNS interventions could achieve their expected impacts.

Table 1.2 Study Areas Selected for Field-Level Data Collection

Geographic locations	Criteria	District	Upazila
1. North/North West	High levels of food insecurity[a]	Nilphamari	Syedpur, Kishoreganj
		Netrokona[b]	Mohanganj, Purbadhala
2. South East	Ethnically mixed area	Cox's Bazar	Chakaria, Ukhyia
3. South West	Coastal area, disaster, or salinity prone	Khulna	Batiaghata, Dakop
		Jessore[b]	Jhikargachha, Chougachha
4. North East	Hilly areas with tea gardens, *haor* areas	Moulavibazar	Srimangal
		Sunamganj	Juri/Dharmapasha[c]

a. All selected areas had the same extent of NNS implementation.
b. Selected only for survey data collection.
c. Dharmapasha upazila in Sunamganj district was chosen for survey data collection instead of Juri. The health facility infrastructure and human resources and the service utilization in Juri were found to be suboptimal because Juri is a new upazila.

Study Sites and Sampling

The national-level interviews were conducted in Dhaka. The district-, upazila-, union-, and community-level data collection was conducted in four districts (table 1.2). These districts were selected from a sampling frame of 150 upazila (in 20 districts) in which NNS reportedly had converted existing IMCI Corners into IMCI and Nutrition (IMCI+N) Corners. The sampling frame was further restricted to 39 upazila in which at least two primary NNS inputs—Basic Nutrition Training and NNS Logistics—reportedly already were in place. This information was derived through discussions with NNS core team members in January–February 2014 about the implementation status. Thus, to provide a good distribution of major geographic, agricultural, and social conditions across Bangladesh, eight upazila were selected from four districts. In addition, Netrokona and Jessore districts in the North and South West regions, respectively, were selected for survey data collection. Therefore, survey data were collected from 12 upazila in 6 districts.

Data Collection

NNS Documents and Implementation Roll-Out Information from IPHN

Information on National Nutrition Service (NNS) operational/implementation plans and draft training manuals was collected from the Institute for Public Health and Nutrition (IPHN) throughout the course of this assessment. Primary documents reviewed for the study were obtained by June 2014. Updated NNS training roll-out data and a comprehensive training plan, a working paper on NNS, and several additional documents were provided to the research team in August 2014.

National-Level Key Informant Interviews

These interviews focused on broad issues of policy, coordination, management, and implementation of nutrition-related services within Bangladesh. Participants selected for an interview were grouped under three broad categories (table 1.3).

Table 1.3 Categories of Interviewees and Number of Interviews at the National Level

Category of interviewee	Number interviewed
NNS core team members	4
Ministry and other policy-level officials	5
Development partners: Multilateral, bilateral, INGO, NGO	8

Note: NNS = National Nutrition Service; INGO = international nongovernmental organization; NGO = nongovernmental organization.

Seventeen key informant interviews were conducted from a selection of these groups of informants. Interviewees were selected in continuing discussions between the core research team and the World Bank contact.

Subnational-Level Data Collection

Qualitative Interviews and Focus Group Discussions

The subnational data collection was carried out in eight upazila across four districts (table 1.4). Districts for subnational qualitative data collection were selected purposively to provide a good distribution of the major geographic, agricultural, and social conditions in Bangladesh within the limitations of the team's research resources. The four districts selected were as follows:

1. Nilphamari, in the North West, a region that experiences high levels of food insecurity
2. Khulna, in the South West, which includes areas frequently affected by cyclones and salinity problems
3. Moulavibazar, in the North East, which includes hilly areas and tea gardens and is ethnically mixed
4. Cox's Bazar, in the South East, which includes a disaster-prone coastal belt.

A team of four field research officers and one supervisor was responsible for qualitative data collection. Table 1.4 provides the number of in-depth interviews and focus group discussions conducted in different upazila with respective dates.

Table A.1 gives the breakdown of the subnational interviewees according to their official capacities in each district. In three districts (Khulna, Nilphamari, and Cox's Bazar), the research team interviewed the civil surgeon. In the fourth (Moulavibazar), the civil surgeon was not available for interview, so the district hospital superintendent was interviewed. In each upazila except Srimangal, the research team interviewed the upazila health and family planning officer (UHFPO), who is the senior medical manager in charge of the upazila health complex. In Srimangal, the UHFPO was on leave so the research team interviewed a residential medical officer (RMO).

Table 1.4 Number of In-Depth Interviews and Focus Group Discussions Conducted in Different Upazila and Collection Dates

District	Upazila	Number of in-depth interviews	Number of focus group discussions	Dates of data collection
Moulavibazar	Srimangal Juri	25	4	May 19–23, 2014
Khulna	Batiaghata Dakop	23	4	May 24–29, 2014
Nilphamari	Syedpur Kishoreganj	22	3	June 1–5, 2014
Cox's Bazar	Chakaria Ukhiya	23	4	June 8–12, 2014

Quantitative Data: Facility Assessments, Service Provider Surveys, and Observations

As noted earlier, quantitative data were collected from 12 upazila in 6 districts (table 1.2). The survey included a facility assessment (to assess training coverage, logistics availability, functioning of IMCI+Nutrition Corner, service utilization), a health care provider survey, observation of case management at IMCI+N Corners and ANC clinics, and an exit interview.

Table 1.5 provides the number of facilities assessed, number of health care providers interviewed, number of observations of case management at IMCI+N Corners and ANC clinics, and exit interviews by survey districts. Exit interviews included the parents/caregivers who had brought a child to the facility for care. Types of instruments used and types of respondents chosen as sources of data collection are presented in table A.2. Characteristics of children and their caregivers are presented in table A.4.

Data Quality Assurance and Processing

Quality Assurance of Field Data Collection

Field data quality was monitored through quality assurance by research investigators from the International Food Policy Research Institute (IFPRI) and the International Centre for Diarrhoeal Disease Research, Bangladesh (ICDDR,B). All questionnaires and data forms were reviewed for accuracy, consistency, and completeness. This review was done immediately after data collection, before the respective research teams left the area. The data collectors made additional field visits to clarify inconsistencies or to collect missing information.

Management and Processing of Qualitative Data

National-level qualitative interviews were conducted in English and, when needed, in Bangla. All of the interviews except one were audio recorded. Once the interviews were completed, the interviewer transcribed the interview in

Table 1.5 Survey Data Collection at Subnational Level by District and Sources of Data Collection

District	Facility assessment	Healthcare provider survey	Antenatal care observation	U5 observation	Exit interviews
Jessore	7	23	210	129	137
Khulna	7	20	33	52	52
Cox's Bazar	6	17	33	223	211
Netrokona	9	19	50	144	138
Nilphamari	7	21	29	119	126
Moulavibazar	5	17	21	89	72
Total	44	122	382	842	816

English from the audio recording. The audio recordings and transcripts then were coded and analyzed using NVivo 10,[1] a computer program for qualitative data analysis.

As with the national-level interviews, all interviews and focus group discussions were audio recorded. Interviews and focus group discussions took up to one hour. Using the audio recordings, summaries of them were written up in Bangla, and then analyzed.

Entering and Cleaning Survey Data

The data entry template for the field-based quantitative data and facility assessments was developed using CSPro. CSPro was preferred because of its comparative advantages over other programs that label variables. Data entry and basic data cleaning were done by Data Analysis and Technical Assistance. Additional data cleaning was done by an IFPRI research analyst. After data cleaning was done, IFPRI, in collaboration with the International Centre for Diarrhoeal Disease Research, Bangladesh (ICDDR,B), did the analysis using Stata 13.

Ethical Approval

Ethical clearance was obtained from the institutional review board (IRB) of the ICDDR,B. IFPRI's IRB designated the ICDDR,B's IRB as the primary IRB for this study. Written and/or oral consent (depending on the interviewee) was obtained before interviews and group discussions.

Note

1. NVivo is a qualitative data analysis program developed by QSR International. See www.qsrinternational.com.

CHAPTER 2

Results

The results of the operational assessment are presented in five sections. Each section covers results on the research domains in table 2.1. Within each results section, the research team drew on the various data sources used to gather data on the domain of inquiry.

Availability of Operational Guidance for National Nutrition Services Intervention Areas

Review of National Nutrition Services (NNS) documents available to the research team revealed that the operational plan (OP) outlines the implementation plans for different NNS interventions (GoB 2011c). Overall, implementation plans have been outlined for all NNS components, including the 13 major components identified as NNS priority areas:

1. Growth monitoring and promotion (GMP)
2. Behavior change communication (BCC)
3. Micronutrient supplementation
4. Control of iodine deficiency disorder (IDD) and salt iodization program
5. Management of severe acute malnutrition (SAM) and community-based management of acute malnutrition (CMAM)
6. Nutrition during emergencies
7. Community-based nutrition services
8. Nutrition interventions in hard-to-reach areas
9. Early childhood development (ECD)
10. Coordination with the Integrated Management of Childhood Illnesses (IMCI) program
11. Climate change and nutrition
12. Geriatric nutrition
13. Noncommunicable diseases (NCDs).

Management and Support Services

Overall, institutional arrangements to deliver NNS interventions using the existing health and family planning infrastructure that delivers nutrition services have been described in specific detail (GoB 2011c). Roles of key NNS staff, line directors, program managers (PMs), and deputy program managers (DPMs) are outlined clearly. The management structure of NNS and operational plan and the major components of the OP and their PMs/DPMs are described, with major activities for which they should be responsible.

The NNS-OP presents the main modalities of the institutional arrangements and modalities of implementation arrangements well. For implementation arrangements, nutrition service delivery at different geographic levels—district, upazila, union, and community—have been identified. Table 2.1 summarizes the implementing authority, implementation support, service providers at different levels, timing of service delivery, and service contents for key components of NNS. Table 2.1 indicates that the OP identified the implementing authority, implementation support, service providers at different levels, timing of service delivery, and service contents for key components of NNS, such as infant and young child feeding (IYCF), GMP, micronutrients, and BCC. However, the OP is missing some of this information for SAM/CMAM.

The implementing authority, implementation support, service providers, timing of service delivery, and service contents for key components of NNS are well described in the Operation Plan and Comprehensive Training Document. The OP includes procurement plans for equipment and furniture for the development of NNS. The OP also includes the action plan to mainstream nutrition services for different target groups; [and] to define the activities, the service delivery (existing and proposed), and the responsibilities (current and proposed). The plan for implementing specific NNS nutrition interventions has been presented in detail with core activities under each intervention, the health workforce responsible, and their Line Directorate.

Table 2.1 Management, Support, and Institutional Arrangements for National Nutrition Services

Key research questions related to management, support, and institutional arrangements	Data sources to address research questions
• Do implementation plans exist for the different interventions?	• Content review of NNS operational documents
• What are the overall institutional arrangements for delivery of NNS interventions through the health system?	• National-level in-depth interviews with NNS staff and other stakeholders in the health system
• How do NNS staff engage with and support planned NNS activities to deliver nutrition results?	• National-level in-depth interviews with other nutrition stakeholders
• Did the supervision and management occur as planned? What is the extent of the intended supervision and management activities?	

Note: NNS = National Nutrition Services.

Box 2.1 What's Working Well in the Management and Support Domains?

Operational Plans

- The OP outlines all components of NNS, including the priority components.
- The institutional arrangements for delivery of NNS interventions using existing health and family planning infrastructure are described in specific detail.
- The management structure of NNS and roles of key NNS staff, line directors, program managers, and deputy program managers (DPM) are outlined clearly.
- Modalities of implementation at different geographic levels are well presented.

Progress in Subnational Coordination

- Most of the subnational interviewees were satisfied with the progress in the coordination of nutrition services and with levels of communication between staff managed by Director General of Health Services (DGHS) and Director General of Family Planning (DGFP) at the upazila level and below.

Although the OP includes an outline of overall planning for all NNS components, the outline does not provide detailed implementation plans and guidelines on how different NNS interventions should be implemented. The research team's assessment is that additional clarity on specific roles of frontline workers and the added activities expected of specific frontline workers for NNS delivery would be helpful.

The OP states that core monitoring and evaluation (M&E) activities include establishing a national resource center on nutrition, establishing a national nutrition surveillance system, and conducting regular nutrition surveys. However, the OP contains no clear plans and guidelines on how these M&E activities will be carried out.

Findings from Qualitative Research on Institutional Arrangements

Table 2.2 shows what emerged to be the most important issues that arose in the *national-level* interviews, in the order of the five major research domains; and within these, in the order of frequency of discussion. Table 2.3 divides these issues of concern among the three broad categories of national-level interviewees to enable some comparison among the three types of stakeholder: NNS core team members; NNS platform, ministry, and policy-level interviewees; and development partners from multilateral and bilateral institutions and nongovernmental organizations (NGOs). The third type included interviewees from the World Bank, United States Agency for International Development (USAID), UK Department for International Development (DFID), United Nations Children's

Table 2.2 Implementing Authority, Implementation Support, Service Providers, Timing of Service Delivery, and Service Contents for Key Components of National Nutrition Services

NNS component	Implementing authority	Implementation support	Service providers at different levels	Timing of service delivery	Service content
IYCF	Specified	Specified	Specified	Specified	Specified
GMP	Specified	Specified	Specified	Specified	Specified
Micronutrients	Partially specified	Specified	Specified	Specified	Specified
BCC	Specified	Specified	Specified	Specified	Specified
SAM/CMAM	Specified	Specified	Not specified	Not specified	Not specified

Note: BCC = behavior change communication; CMAM = community-based management of acute malnutrition; GMP = Growth Monitoring and Promotion; IYCF = infant and young child feeding; SAM = severe acute malnutrition.

Table 2.3 Main Issues Raised under Each Research Domain and Relative Emphasis Given to Each Issue in the National-Level Interviews

		Number of times issue is cited in interviews as important			
Domain	Issue raised	Number of total interviews (N = 17)	NNS core team members (N = 4)	NNS platform, ministry, and policy-level participants (N = 5)	Development partners (N = 8)
Management and support services	IPHN overall capacity, authority, leadership, and coordination	16	4	5	7
	Need for more time for NNS to become embedded in the existing infrastructure	15	4	5	6
	Capacity in NNS	14	4	4	6
	Continuity in NNS leadership	14	1	5	8
	Coordination and communication among DG Health, DG Family Planning, and other ministries	13	2	5	6
	Procurement of logistics and supplies	12	2	5	5
	Field visits and communication between NNS in Dhaka and upazila and community clinics	11	3	3	5
	Problems in NNS budgets and auditing	10	3	3	4
	Recruitment and retention of frontline workers, including medical officers (MOs)	5	1	3	1
	Recruitment and retention of other NNS staff (PMs and DPMs)	4	3	1	0

table continues next page

Table 2.3 Main Issues Raised under Each Research Domain and Relative Emphasis Given to Each Issue in the National-Level Interviews *(continued)*

Domain	Issue raised	Number of total interviews (N = 17)	NNS core team members (N = 4)	NNS platform, ministry, and policy-level participants (N = 5)	Development partners (N = 8)
			Number of times issue is cited in interviews as important		
	Influence on, and ability to coordinate and communicate with, other key ministries (such as Food, Agriculture, Livestock and Fisheries, Women and Children's Affairs, Disaster Management)	4	0	2	2
Training and capacity development	Preparation of training materials	15	4	5	6
	Follow-up and supervision after training frontline staff	5	3	1	1
	Organizing training courses, including budget approval	4	2	1	1
Delivery of services	Frontline worker workloads	12	4	3	5
	Frontline staff: Incentives, motivation, and staff numbers	10	2	4	4
	Community-based mechanisms for creating awareness and demand for nutrition services	7	3	2	2
Monitoring and evaluation	M&E	15	4	5	6
	Management information: Indicators, record keeping, compilation, and review	13	4	3	6

Note: DPM = deputy program manager; IPHN = Institute for Public Health and Nutrition; M&E = monitoring and evaluation; NNS = National Nutrition Services; PM = program manager.

Fund (UNICEF), Food and Agriculture Organization of the United Nations (FAO), and Save Children.

Table 2.4 breaks down the issues of concern that were raised in the *subnational* interviews and focus group discussions, disaggregated according to types of post occupied by the interviewees or participants at district and upazila levels. Table 2.3 focuses primarily on district and upazila health leadership and medical officers. Similar information on issues of concern raised in the interviews of frontline providers at upazila, union, and community levels are provided in table A.3. The issues raised in the interviews are organized under the five research domains that guided the current study. Results presented under each of these domains are the most important and frequently raised issues of concern that arose in these interviews and focus group discussions.

Table 2.3 and table 2.4 summarize the major issues that emerged from the qualitative interviews in this section. However, the research team focuses on the insights that are relevant to Domain 1: issues of management, programmatic support, and institutional arrangements.

Table 2.4 Frequency of Issues Discussed as Important in Subnational-Level Interviews with Health Officials at District and Upazila Levels

		Official post of interviewee			
Domain	Issue raised by interviewee as important	Civil surgeon/ District superintendent (N = 4)	Upazila health and family planning officer (N = 7)	Upazila family planning officer (N = 8)	Medical officer/ Residential medical officer (N = 9)
Management and support services	Is there a need for better communication and coordination?	Yes: 4	Yes: 6, No: 1	Yes: 8	Yes: 6
	Is there a problem with retention of medical officers?	Yes: 4	Yes: 5	Yes: 1	Yes: 4
	Is there a problem due to demand for curative services?	Yes: 3	Yes: 4	Yes: 1	Yes: 8
Training and capacity development	Received nutrition training through NNS?	Yes: 2	Yes: 1, No: 6	Yes: 4, No: 4	Yes: 1, No: 8
	Received ToT through NNS?	Yes: 2	Yes: 1, No: 3	Yes: 1	No: 2
	Is there a lack of follow-up supervision after training?	Yes: 2, No: 1	Yes: 2, No: 1	Yes: 1	No: 4
	Is there a lack of clarity about NNS (apart from BCC)?	Yes: 2, No: 1	Yes: 2, No: 5	Yes:1, No: 6	Yes: 3, No: 2
Delivery of nutrition services	Are preventive services being crowded out by demand for curative services?	Yes: 1, No: 1	Yes: 4	Yes: 5	Yes: 9
	Is there a lack of medicine or supplement supply?	No: 3	Yes: 5, No: 1	Yes: 2, No: 1	Yes: 8
	Is treatment of malnutrition (SAM/MAM) inadequate?	Yes: 2, No: 2	Yes: 3, No: 2	Yes: 2	Yes: 4, No: 1

table continues next page

Table 2.4 Frequency of Issues Discussed as Important in Subnational-Level Interviews with Health Officials at District and Upazila Levels (continued)

Domain	Issue raised by interviewee as important	Official post of interviewee			
		Civil surgeon/ District superintendent (N = 4)	Upazila health and family plan- ning officer (N = 7)	Upazila family planning officer (N = 8)	Medical officer/ Residential medical officer (N = 9)
Monitoring and evaluation	Is there a lack of clar- ity about monitoring requirements?	Yes: 4	Yes: 4, No: 1	Yes: 6	Yes: 2, No: 1
	Is there a lack of M&E tools?	No: 1	Yes: 3	Yes: 1	Yes: 1
	Is any M&E conducted for nutrition inputs?	—	No: 2	No: 1	Yes: 2, No: 1
Exposure to inter- ventions	Has coverage improved after the establishment of CCs?	Yes: 3	Yes: 6	Yes: 7	Yes: 3
	Are upazila health com- plexes (UHCs) prevented from providing ade- quate nutrition services due to poor staffing?	Yes: 2	Yes: 5	No: 4	Yes: 8

Note: BCC = behavior change communication; CCs = community clinics; M&E = monitoring and evaluation; MAM = management of acute malnutrition; NNS = National Nutrition Services; SAM = severe acute malnutrition; ToT = training of trainers.

The research team's assessment of the institutional functioning and management of NNS drew mainly from the national-level interviews. These focused primarily on broad policy issues, the management of NNS, and the overall progress made in the implementation and coordination of services.

Capacity in NNS Not Assessed in Advance

Capacity challenges within NNS were raised by all three categories of interviewees and in 14 of the 17 interviews. When the NNS-OP was published, it showed that NNS was to be implemented from Institute for Public Health and Nutrition (IPHN). However, there was no appraisal of IPHN's capacity to handle such a big budget program. In fact, an analysis of the utilization of funds released indicates low rates of use (figure 2.1).

It seems that whether NNS management staff had all the these capacities had not been considered. For example, most of the development partner interviewees pointed out that NNS staff nearly always asked for technical support from other stakeholders, including development partners, to produce documents and modules because the NNS staff did not have the capacity to produce them "in house." Figure 2.1 highlights the low rate of utilization of funds allocated to NNS. In Year 1, BDT 24.47 crore (or almost 38 percent) of the funds were not used.

Figure 2.1 Allocation and Usage of Funds for FY2011/12 and First Six Months of 2012/13

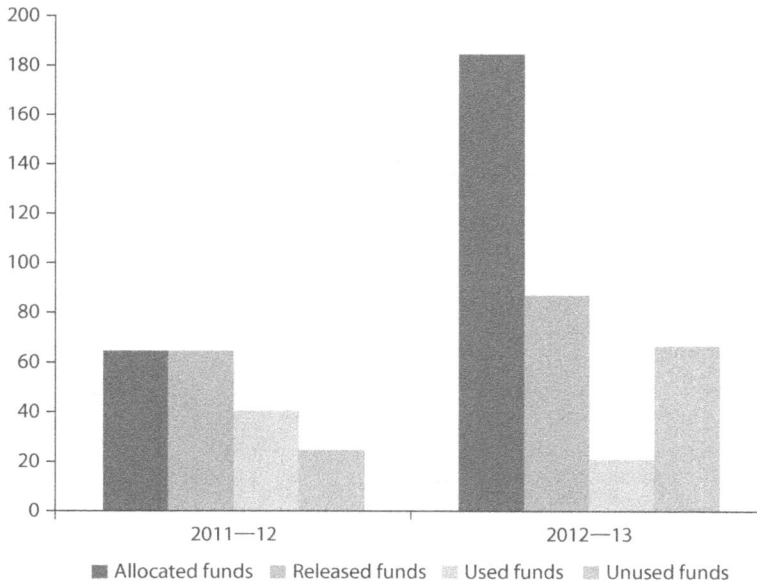

Source: GoB, n.d., NNS implementation status report, internal and unpublished.

Expenditure data for Year 2 is available for only the first six months. However, the data available indicate that only 25 percent of the released funds were utilized.

Some interviewees raised questions about the capacity of NNS line directors. NNS platform interviewees noted that some line directors were brought in who had no experience with, or exposure to, nutrition issues. This lack of experience meant that these directors were limited in their ability to handle the program effectively. This constraint, in turn, had a negative impact on the work and also indicated that NNS was not being properly regarded at the more senior government levels.

One NNS core team member reported:

> No one explored the readiness of this office in handling this big budget OP. There was no prior assessment whether the staff here had the capacity to handle such a big budget and whether the accounts system had the capacity to manage it. Nothing was assessed.

Continuity in NNS Leadership Essential

Almost all of the interviewees discussed the way that frequent changes in the leadership of IPHN, and thus NNS, had hampered the ability of NNS to progress in mainstreaming nutrition services. IPHN houses NNS and is supposed to coordinate with the different directorates that implement NNS in the field. Thus, leadership for NNS is supposed to come from the IPHN. However, the line director for NNS also is the IPHN Director. Unfortunately, there have been five different IPHN

Directors with fairly brief tenures during the past three years. Most national-level respondents said that, as a result, IPHN had lacked consistent leadership. These absences of leadership hindered its work, particularly in coordinating nutrition services with other directorates and ministries, but also its own implementation of services, such as in developing training modules. These respondents felt that if a line director did not stay for more than six months, NNS would not move forward. *Continuity in leadership was seen as essential* (a) for the director to grasp the work that was going on and (b) for the other staff to get accustomed to the management system introduced by that director.

There also seemed to be a pattern that some new line directors were brought in immediately prior to their retirement. This pattern led to their leaving quickly. Many interviewees thought that this pattern indicated that IPHN was not considered sufficiently important in higher government levels.

One NNS platform member interviewee expressed the problem thus:

> *IPHN is falling behind in providing training. They were supposed to produce modules in the first year, but this was not done on time and afterwards things were falling behind with training. The reason behind this is the problem with NNS leadership. If a line director does not stay for even six months, then how can [that person] move forward? Continuity is essential. As for me, I have been doing this work for five years and have reached somewhere. Now I have a clear understanding and so do my colleagues. But if I changed every few months, this would cost time lost in orientation itself.*

Other interviewees from all three categories expressed strongly how the lack of continuity in NNS leadership was hampering the progress of the program.

From a development partner:

> *NNS is a problem area now and strong leadership is needed. That person should stay for the long term and not be coming and going.*

Another NNS platform participant expressed concerns about the lack of long-term leadership at IPHN:

> *Actually, if you look at the history, then you will see only a few times [that] IPHN was directed by the right person. Many times a person here was sent right prior to his retirement. [IPHN] was never treated as an important organization. Those who had been working in the organization for a long time had to deal with new directors who were brought in from outside, who might not have a nutrition-biased attitude. For various reasons, IPHN did not reach the expected standard.*

Coordination and Communication among Director General of Health Services, Director General of Family Planning, and Other Ministries Is Essential

The complex nature of nutrition services in Bangladesh makes coordination and communication among the various government ministries and development partners essential (figure 2.2). Many of the national-level interviewees expressed

Figure 2.2 Major Components of National Nutrition Services Operational Plan and Their Program Managers and Deputy Program Manager

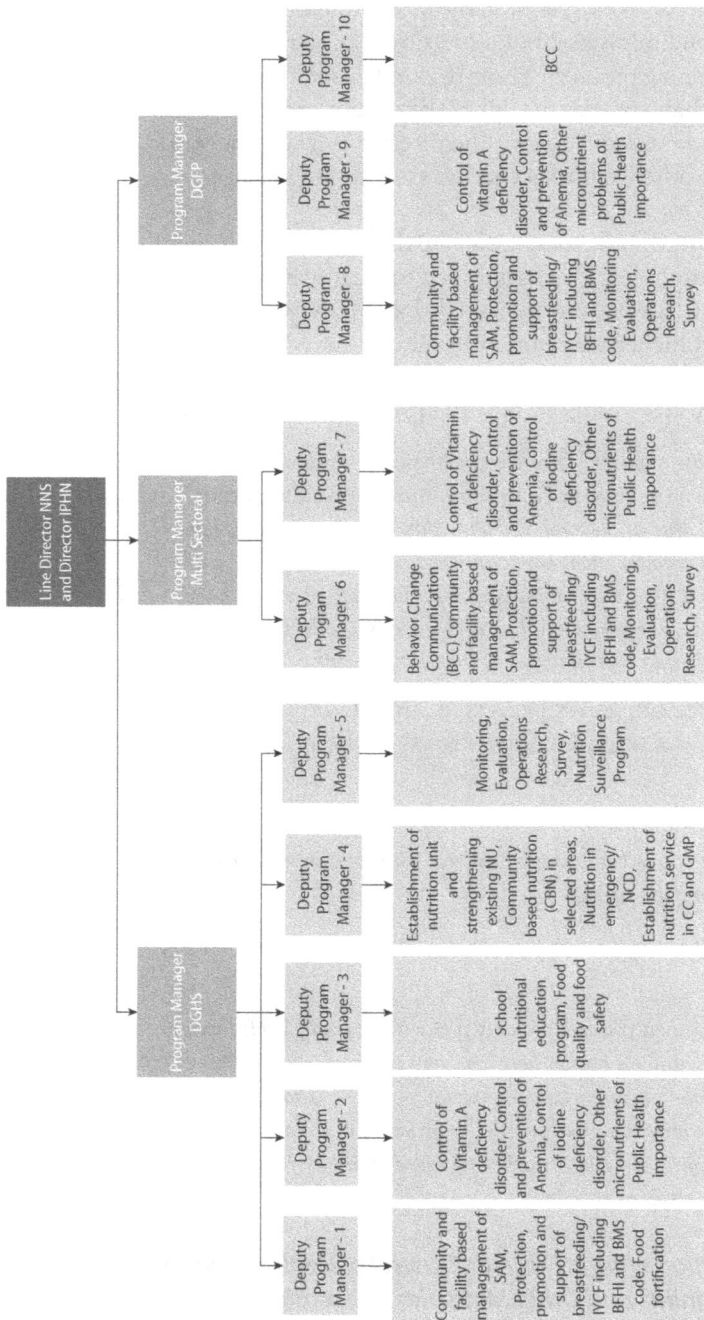

Note: BFHI = Baby-Friendly Hospital Initiatve; BMS = breast milk substitutes; DGFP = Director General of Family Planning; DGHS = Director General of Health Services; GMP = Growth Monitoring and Promotion; IPHN = Institute for Public Health and Nutrition; IYCF = infant and young child feeding; NCD = noncommunicable disease; NNS = National Nutrition Services; NU = nutrition unit; SAM = severe acute malnutrition.

frustration about a lack of communication and coordination—particularly at senior levels.

One NNS platform member expressed frustration with the way that ministries tend to be compartmentalized:

> If you see a basic nutrition problem, then you see it is not possible to holistically achieve anything by putting responsibility on one ministry. It should be the responsibility of various ministries. The World Bank tried a lot to help coordinate all these ministries. But this is a very complex thing. Moreover we have a structural problem in our country. All the ministries are very compartmentalized and it is difficult for them to create any linkage with each another. It is not possible for one ministry to overcome this structural problem.

Another development partner discussed how challenging she/he believed it was for NNS director to facilitate coordination between DGHS and DGFP:

> At this senior level, to say we expect others to report to IPHN on what they are doing in nutrition. The IPHN director cannot go like a beggar to the door of the other OPs and beg them for their information, begging them, "Please mainstream, please do this." There is DGFP: "Oh, we are thinking of mainstreaming." I want to ask, "Why are you thinking about it? Why aren't you doing it through the country? IPHN and NNS are providing you the technical support." The NNP days are gone. Still now DGHS and DGFP are wondering what NNS is doing around nutrition, when they actually should be looking here: "Am I doing what I should be doing on nutrition?" And they are not.

Development partners also stressed that the IPHN director often does not have sufficient power within government to drive through the changes that are needed to make NNS successful as a cross-cutting program.

One development partner expressed it thus:

> When the Director General of Health Services presides over meetings, line directors take nutrition seriously and it gets importance. So an authoritative, powerful figure needs to preside over the meeting.

And from another development partner:

> The line director of NNS can coordinate, but the accountability has to come from somebody above. I don't hear much of that happening. I think NNS gets blamed for things that are not necessarily under [its] control.

Another challenge with coordination is among staff from the two directorates within NNS itself. For example, several DPMs are responsible for different components of NNS' IF component. This arrangement of same/similar interventions being managed by multiple DPMs, and across directorates requires regular, efficient coordination among the directorates and thus could add challenges for the DPMs to coordinate. Difficulties with coordination could delay decision making and implementation of NNS interventions.

*Influence On, and Ability to Coordinate and Communicate with, Other Key
Government Sectors such as Food, Agriculture, Livestock and Fisheries, Women and
Children's Affairs, and Disaster Management*
National-level interviewees raised the issue of NNS needing to coordinate and
communicate with other key government sectors that work on nutrition. The
mandate of NNS is to promote, integrate, and monitor nutrition services horizon-
tally across a range of sectors. However, government sectors tend to be authoritarian
in management style and vertically segmented. Many national-level interviewees
said that the facilitation of intragovernmental collaboration cannot come from
NNS alone, but must be actively promoted at senior levels in all relevant sectors.
Collaboration is happening to some extent. Nevertheless, NNS needs to be better
linked to all nutrition-related activities so that clear and internally consistent messages about nutrition are provided by all relevant government officers.

One NNS core team member stated:

> *Our information system will remain. The unit is a stopgap but the system is working
> and that matters. If the community clinics and FWCs can provide services effectively,
> then nutrition will be addressed. I am very hopeful about our multi-sector approach
> that does not provide services at the field. But all ministries need to work together and
> coordination needs to be improved. Every ministry needs to identify its own nutrition
> activity and make an action plan to implement and this coordination is essential. This
> is the most essential thing for me. This is a challenge and another mammoth task.
> Struggling with managing my own group and involving 13 ministries is hard.*

Communication and Coordination with Subnational Staff
Most of the subnational interviewees were satisfied with progress in coordination
of nutrition services and with levels of communication between staff managed
by DGHS and DGFP at the upazila level and below. Communications with NNS
staff based in Dhaka were problematic. Letters were not answered, and requests
for logistics supplies were ignored for long periods.

Time Required for Nutrition Services to Become Embedded in the Existing Infrastructure

Several national-level interviewees from all categories pointed out that after the
inception of NNS in 2011, implementation was delayed because of lack of
readiness and absence of staff. However, most interviewees from the NNS core
team and many NNS platform participants were more optimistic about recent
progress. Development partner interviewees also pointed out that support and
information systems needed to be in place in the initial stages of the program,
but had not been there. Presently, they felt that these systems were much more
developed and that the program could roll out more easily.

One NNS core team member shared:

> *After 10 years I want to see that breast-feeding will be 100 percent successful and IYCF
> will be at least 60–70 percent successful. We hope we will reach that target through the way*

we are working now. Initially it takes time for a program to pick up speed but, later, it runs smoothly. Now we are fast, our work is running now. Earlier it was just walking slowly.

A government line director of health mentioned:

We have started nutritional activities in Bangladesh by mainstreaming nutrition. It might have taken a little longer in the conceptualization. But if we can handle this effectively and efficiently, then, of course, we will be able to improve nutrition of the country, because we have the system and human resources. We will be able to bring change, but it will require a little more time.

Recruitment and Retention of Other NNS Staff (PMs and DPMs)

Three interviewees raised concerns about delayed recruitment of deputy project managers (DPMs). NNP had had a different set of management staff whom we understood did not transfer directly into NNS. Inherited staff consisted more of junior support staff such as office attendants. There has been a high turnover in management staff since the start of NNS, with 10 of 13 PM and DPM posts having had staff changes. As with the problem with continuity in the overall NNS directorship, this high level of turnover within management posts impedes the success of the program.

Workload for NNS Managers

Many of the national-level interviewees also expressed concerns about the way that workloads were managed within IPHN—particularly the workloads of PMs and DPMs. A great deal of management, coordination, and monitoring is required to get a complex, cross-cutting program such as NNS to be effective. However, it seems that these staff were not able to devote sufficient time to manage the program nor to go to the field to monitor frontline implementation firsthand. Instead, they seemed to be overburdened with bureaucratic requirements and negotiations and needed to attend a large number of meetings and seminars in Dhaka—including those initiated by development partners. To deal with these problems, as suggested by some interviewees, better long-term leadership at IPHN and better coordination with other government officials and development partners will be required.

One development partner interviewee stated the problem thus:

To be honest, in IPHN there are people who are working and there are people who are not. There is a kind of acceptance that there are a certain number of people who are going to do something and there are those who will not. There are several policies, strategies in the curricula that are there for months, but haven't moved anywhere. I don't know if IPHN is understaffed or staff within IPHN are not managed appropriately. I don't know what the issue is, but there are [a] few people in IPHN who pretty much do everything. It's just impossible to attend all of the meetings and do all the things the entire unit is supposed to do. I don't know, but it could be they are understaffed or there are a lot of staff who are not doing what they could be doing. But there is not a whole lot of good personnel management.

Problems in NNS Budgets and Auditing

All of the core NNS team interviewees and a number of the development partner interviewees reported that, in the first year at least, it had been very difficult to spend the allocated budget. Several reasons were given. Most agreed that, initially, NNS itself was not able to cope with such a large budget—particularly in accounts capability and in human resources. Second, training modules took longer than expected to prepare, delaying training sessions. Finally, employment of multipurpose volunteers—which was supposed to have been 33 percent of the budget—was not approved.

One NNS platform interviewee discussed how NNS-OP came with a big budget. While the large budget could have been seen as a reflection of the government's good intentions regarding nutrition, NNS staff were not ready to handle it. In hindsight, it seems unfortunate that such a large budget was allocated to NNS in the first year of operations, when the institutional capacity to cope with it was not yet fully established. The team research team recommends that, in future, in the initial stages of implementation, budgets will be more flexible.

In addition, NNS core team interviewees talked about how they failed to spend the allocated amount of money for each year. In the first year, because training modules and guidelines were not in place, NNS was unable to carry out the targeted number of trainings. As a result, money was unspent and returned. Government policy determined that NNS received the following year's budget based on the amount spent in the previous year, not on NNS's proposal for the upcoming year. This continued underspending created an ongoing budget problem.

More than half of the interviewees also talked about the crisis they faced with audits in Year 1. One NNS core team member, two platform members, and one development partner interviewee drew attention to irregularities in the auditing of NNS accounts. One negative outcome of these irregularities was that NNS core team members were forced to devote excessive attention to dealing with auditing problems. In addition, morale among NNS staff declined, and goodwill with other cooperating partners was undermined. All of these difficulties combined to hinder the progress of NNS activities.

Summary of Findings on Design and Institutional Arrangements

The document review and interviews with diverse stakeholders raised the following key issues related to program design and to institutional arrangements for delivering on NNS interventions.

Program Design

Two central issues emerge in relation to the design of NNS program: (1) the challenge of lack of focus or specificity in choosing the number of interventions to deliver through NNS and (2) the choice of intervention platforms to achieve the full reach of the DNIs. The research team's analysis is that these two issues have led to a very large number of interventions to be coordinated and delivered by NNS.

The research highlighted that there likely are too many intervention areas in the original OP for NNS to deal effectively with in the required time span. A smaller set of interventions to mainstream could have enabled a clearer focus on implementation needs for each intervention-delivery platform combination.

Institutional Capacity and Governance Issues

The research team's results indicate that *maintaining strong and stable leadership is the essential element to ensure integrated and well-coordinated comprehensive service delivery by NNS*. As noted earlier, the NNS line director also is the IPHN Director. This arrangement apparently was unable to foster effective implementation and coordination of NNS because of the difficulties in recruiting and retaining the Director of IPHN and that individual's limited technical expertise in nutrition.

These two difficulties are compounded by the inability of the IPHN director who was also an NNS line director to ensure effective coordination with other line directors, given their position at the same grade level. A careful examination and discussion within the government and among stakeholders to identify a leadership solution for NNS coordination is crucial to NNS' success. The research team sees *creating the conditions for proactive and consistent NNS leadership as the most fundamental and serious challenge for a cross-sectoral initiative such as NNS*.

Additional significant capacity- and workload-related challenges within NNS/IPHN hampered effective implementation of NNS. Two of those identified were NNS capacity challenges related to developing (a) feasible and specific implementation plans for the intervention delivery and (b) careful training approaches to maintain and manage records on the training roll-out, and to manage budgets as large as that for NNS (table 2.5). Consultation with NNS DPMs also revealed coordination and communication gaps among NNS core team members. Addressing some of these gaps would help ensure that NNS managers could

Table 2.5 Training and Capacity Development

Key research questions related to training and capacity development	Data sources
• What are the institutional arrangements for training for each NNS intervention?	• Content review of NNS operational documents and upazila-level records
• To what extent have training and performance improvement measures been rolled out for all NNS interventions?	• National-level in-depth interviews with NNS staff and other stakeholders in the health system
• To what extent have NNS staff and implementing staff from the health system been exposed to NNS training and performance improvement inputs?	• National-level in-depth interviews with other nutrition stakeholders
• Did the training occur as intended and to what extent? What is the participation and engagement of trainers and recipients in the training?	• Service provider surveys

Note: NNS = National Nutrition Services.

devote more time to managing the program and less time to other tasks, such as negotiating with bureaucracy and attending meetings. It also was clear that much could be gained, for both managers and frontline workers, if NNS managers (PMs and DPMs) took more time to visit frontline service delivery workers in the field.

Development partners certainly could support some of these institutional capacity challenges. However, it is not clear that there is a clear "drawdown" strategy for development partner support to NNS. This strategy is another area that needs additional careful consideration.

Findings on Training from Review of National Nutrition Services Operational Documents

Various forms of training, orientation, and capacity-building activities have been identified as priorities for NNS to enhance its (human and institutional) capacities, as well as those of other Line Directorates that have responsibilities for delivering nutrition services. These activities are:

1. Job training (preservice).
2. In-service training.
3. Orientation (on nutrition activities).
4. Joint training (to ensure synergy among health, family planning, and field-workers of other departments that deliver nutrition activities; development of understanding and team spirit to deliver good services).
5. Specific program and theme-based training (training on IYCF, management of malnutrition, adolescent nutrition, nutrition counselling, micronutrients, and emerging problems will be given to the PMs, who then will train the staffs of their working areas).
6. Workshop/seminars/conferences.
7. Overseas training for doctors and nurses.

For staff training at different levels of NNS delivery, the OP provides overall plans that cover major topics, potential participants, and duration of training. Training topics included are as follows:

1. Mainstreaming nutrition.
2. Maternal nutrition.
3. Infant and young child feeding (IYCF).
4. Severe acute malnutrition (SAM) and community-based management of acute malnutrition (CMAM).

The OP also provides a training plan that outlines a list of trainings with estimated costs. The list includes the training topics, potential participants, number of batches, number of trainees, duration of training, geographic locations (central, district, or upazila level), and estimated costs. The description of the training process is detailed in the Comprehensive Training Plan.

The master trainers are envisaged as training of trainers (ToT) resource persons and, eventually, the ToT for the Basic Nutrition Training for field service providers. However, there is no description in the manual of the profile and selection process of the resource persons for the master trainer orientation and how the training will cascade from the central to the peripheral levels of the health system.

The research team's review of the NNS Training Manual (GoB 2013a) revealed the following issues:

- Contents of the manual
  - The training manual resembles a guideline for the facilitators who should conduct training for the basic training for field service providers. The training format, methods, set-up and requirements, and training schedule are detailed for each session. Learning objectives of each session are clearly outlined. However, the contents of the training module, such as the IYCF module, seem too extensive for community-level health care providers to complete in four days.
  - Some information/material on general nutrition, undernutrition, and growth monitoring needs to be more specific for the level of expertise of the intended participants (such as community health workers, or CHW). The manual could be simplified for CHWs.
  - The visual aids are not adequate to present examples of SAM or management of acute malnutrition (MAM). The quality of pictures in the manual is not high, and some pictures are blurred.
  - The basic training manual for field service providers should be simpler, with more specific information.
  - Classroom training may be followed by field practice for two to three days that should build confidence in field service providers and enhance learning by identifying and clarifying mistakes by supervisors.

- Learning activities
  - The manual uses a variety of teaching methods, including presentations, group assignments, poster presentations, and practical sessions. However, it might also be useful to include opportunities for trainees to share experiences regarding nutrition service delivery.

- Participant evaluation
  - The training manual contains tools for pre- and postevaluation of the trainees. The manual also includes a form to evaluate the training. However, the manual does not suggest possible follow-up activities with participants and next steps for learning and development. Refresher training sessions could be included in the training plan. These sessions could be offered quarterly on selected topics focusing on one or more NNS component.
  - The training manuals are being revised but, to the research team's knowledge, the revisions include no documented, structured identification of nutritional capacity gaps and assessment of training needs and effectiveness.

Box 2.2   What's Working Well in Training and Capacity Development?

Training Manuals

- Training manuals are in place for Basic Nutrition Training, IYCF training, and SAM management.
- Basic Nutrition Training manuals are being revised.

Training
Basic Nutrition Training and logistics support for delivery of NNS are under way after considerable delays during the first year of operations.

- Training of trainers (ToT) by master trainers is almost complete across all upazila.
- Trainers at the upazila level in turn have started conducting training of field service providers in interventions laid out in the Basic Nutrition Training package.

Findings from National Nutrition Services Implementation Roll-Out Data

The research team used a list of 150 NNS implementation upazila made available by NNS to the team in early 2014 for its initial assessments of training roll-out. The team presented the initial results in August 2014. Then, based on discussions with NNS team, the team attempted to build additional information into this datasheet on actual dates of implementation and support available for implementation by other partners. As noted earlier, it was not possible to obtain this information in a comprehensive manner so the process of collating the information for this datasheet was challenging.

The research team's current assessment is that NNS roll-out is characterized by scaling up a series of training and other support inputs to districts and upazila to enable the health system to put in place a diverse set of nutrition-related activities within the current set of health system activities. These training and support inputs include the following:

1. *Basic Nutrition Training.* Basic Nutrition Training is an extensive training for field-level health workers. It contains 18 sessions, each lasting one to two hours. Session topics include food and nutrition, micronutrients, nutrition for different age groups, GMP, food security/quality/safety, nutrition in emergencies, IYCF, BCC, counselling techniques, MS Excel operation, and email communications.
2. *NNS logistics training/input.* NNS logistics include the provision of equipment necessary to provide services in NNS framework. This equipment includes mid-upper arm circumference (MUAC) tape, weighing machines, and height scale.
3. *SAM training.* SAM training is a comprehensive training on managing severely malnourished children. This training is divided in nine modules, which start

with general ideas on nutrition and expand to different topics, such as SAM management principles, community outreach, tracking an individual child, and community-level monitoring.

Additional information on the training roll-out was made available to the research team in August 2014. These data indicate that, between 2012 and 2014, Basic Nutrition Training was completed by NNS in 210 upazila (81 completed in 2012, 82 in 2014) (table 2.6). NNS logistics inputs, which include provision of equipment, such as weighing scales, and support/training on the use of the equipment, have been somewhat slower to roll out. Last available data suggest that 131 upazila received NNS logistics, all in 2013. Additional analysis shows that the number of upazila receiving both Basic Nutrition Training and logistics was only 101. Of these, 30 upazila received the logistics but no nutrition training; and 110 upazila did not receive logistics after the basic training. A potential reason behind these gaps is the MoHFW's decision to couple logistics input with the Global Alliance for Vaccines and Immunization (GAVI) training program, instead of with NNS training. Implementation of SAM training has been the most rapid among all types of NNS training packages. To date, SAM training has been completed in 319 upazila.

Table C1 shows the number of health service providers who received the ToT in the first 18 months of NNS implementation (to December 2012, the last date available from NNS). The findings indicate that, even though all other NNS training had been cascaded to some extent, CMAM training had yet to be cascaded after the first 18 months of implementation.

Figure 2.3 Number of Upazila Receiving Their First Training, by Year, 2012–14

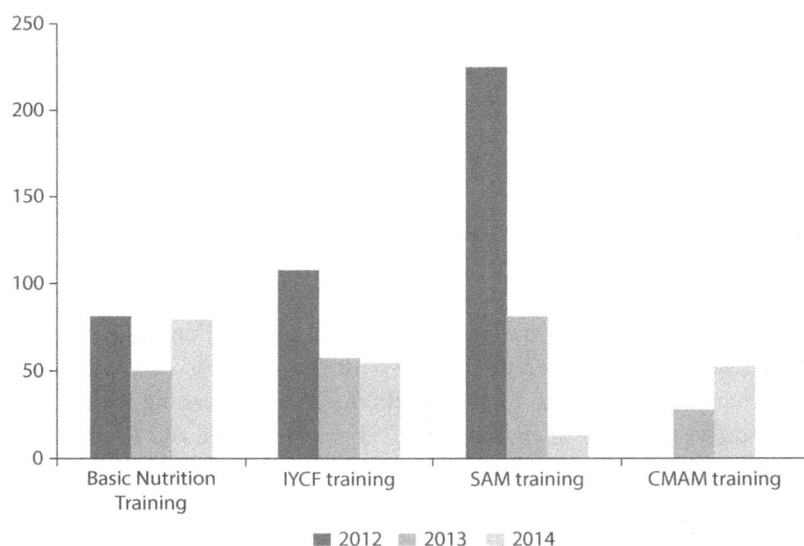

Source: GoB, n.d., NNS implementation status report, internal and unpublished.
Note: CMAM = community-based management of acute malnutrition; IYCF = infant and young child feeding; SAM = severe acute malnutrition.

Table 2.6 Types of NNS Training/Inputs and Their Implementation Status, by Year, 2012–14

Types of training/NNS inputs	No. of upazila			Total no. of upazila in which NNS training/input has been provided to date
	2012	2013	2014	
Basic Nutrition Training	81[a]	50	82	210[a]
NNS logistics input	0	131	0	131
SAM	225	82	60	319[a]
All trainings/inputs for NNS delivery[b]	n.a.	n.a.	n.a.	66

Note: NNS = National Nutrition Services; SAM = severe acute malnutrition.
a. Row totals will not add up because, in a few upazila, a particular training was conducted multiple times.
b. In table 2.4, "All trainings/inputs" refers to Basic Nutrition Training, NNS logistics, and SAM training.

Figure 2.4 Upazila Receiving NNS Trainings in Each Division

percent

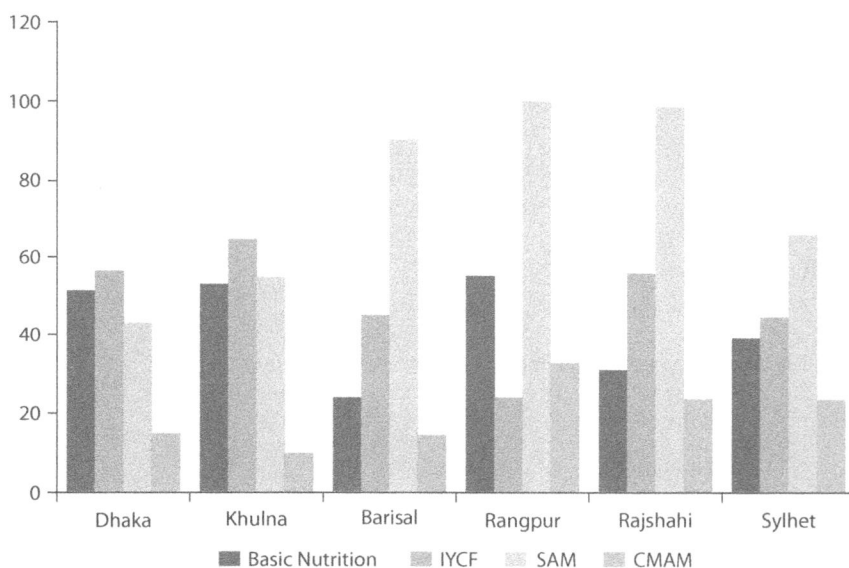

Source: GoB, n.d., NNS implementation status report, internal and unpublished.
Note: CMAM = community-based management of acute malnutrition; IYCF = infant and young child feeding; SAM = severe acute malnutrition.

Figure 2.4 shows the extent of training implementation in different divisions in Bangladesh. Barisal division lags behind in Basic Nutrition Training. The percentage of upazila receiving this training is highest in Rajshahi. SAM training is the most commonly conducted training in each division except for Dhaka and Khulna.

Based on the 150 upazila implementation roll-out data that initially were received from NNS, to conduct this operational assessment, we chose a subset of 12 upazila in which key roll-out activities were completed. Thus, the results in this report should be seen as reflecting the state of implementation in these upazila.

Findings from National-Level Interviews on NNS Training, Capacity, and Roll-Out

The national-level interviews highlighted key challenges within the training and roll-out processes about preparation of training materials and follow-up and supervision after training, procurement of logistics and supplies, recruitment, and retention of frontline workers.

Preparation of Training Materials

Preparation of training materials reportedly was slow during the initial stages of the program so held up implementation. Some NNS core interviewees said that preparing the training materials took a long time because very little had been inherited from the previous program, the National Nutrition Program (NNP). It was not clear to the research team as to why so little had been inherited. Many of the development partners were frustrated by the very slow progress of the training materials preparation. More recently, it seems that NNS is making progress and modules have been developed, but much more progress is needed.

Follow-up and Supervision after Training

Development partners spoke about the need to check and reinforce what had been learned in nutrition training so nutrition services and counselling were included in services provided by frontline health and family planning workers. Because monitoring and information only recently had been compiled and reviewed, it was not yet clear how much of this follow-up on-the-job supervision was taking place.

Organizing Training Courses: Multiple Delays

Additional delays were added by the slowness of recruitment of PMs and DPMs within IPHN. Furthermore, training modules were prepared with others stakeholders' inputs, which were delayed. Finally, concerns were raised about the lack of clarity on how training was to be implemented at different levels.

Procurement of Logistics and Supplies

Two NNS core team members raised concerns about logistics and medicine supply problems, including the liaisoning with the Central Medical Stores Depot (CMSD). The NNS platform interviewees did not think that there were problems with logistics and medical supplies. Development partner interviewees had mixed responses about logistics and supplies. Three interviewees from this category did not think they were a problem, but two interviewees were concerned about logistics delays and nearly expired medicines being sent from central stores.

Recruitment and Retention o Frontline Workers, Including MOs

The need to recruit frontline workers was raised in a number of interviews. The current workloads of health assistants (HAs), family welfare volunteers (FWVs), family welfare assistants (FWAs), and community health care providers (CHCPs) were high. Furthermore, if these workers were not on post, or were moving there after they had received training, the implementation of NNS was hindered. Therefore, efforts to improve timely recruitment and retention of key frontline staff also should improve NNS implementation.

The widespread problem of medical officers (MOs) absenteeism at the upazila level was another key issue raised in both national-level and subnational-level interviews. These officers are the ones most often trained as trainers in the ToT program. However, it was reported that they often used the opportunity afforded them by Dhaka-based training to enhance their careers while in Dhaka, which led them to spend time away from their posts in upazila health complexes. The problem of MOs neglecting upazila posts is not easily resolved. NNS may need to consider approaches to cope with this widespread problem, perhaps by not relying so strongly on this cadre, particularly in the ToT program.

Perspectives from Subnational Stakeholders on Training, Capacity, and Roll-Out

In-depth interviews with the health care providers revealed that most frontline staff had received nutrition training of some kind in the past, but were unable to tell whether it was linked with NNS. The assessment of training across the many levels of frontline staff was very complex. Many of the training courses that had been attended by frontline staff had nutrition components—for example, in IYCF-, IMCI-, and NGO-organized training courses. However, we found very little evidence of specific nutrition training among frontline staff in health or family planning, despite the fact that the upazila were chosen as areas that had received NNS training. The complexity of training provision creates a challenge for NNS in its responsibility to provide, coordinate, and monitor nutrition nutrition for frontline health and family planning staff.

Results from qualitative interviews revealed various problems associated with training courses. There was some evidence of training courses not being carried out properly or not lasting for the number of days they were supposed to take. One UFPO said that she/he had gone to a two-day training, but the course was finished in only one day. Other courses were supposed to last all day, but were finished by noon.

In-depth interviews with health care providers at the subnational level highlighted concerns about the gap between training and practice. HAs and FWAs face many practical problems in the field. They also often receive specific training courses associated with one part of their work responsibility, such as IMCI, IYCF, and Expanded Program of Immunization (EPI). However, apart from their basic training, they do not receive much guidance on how to combine all these disparate courses in their work. As a result, because of high workloads, it is difficult for these workers to combine all of these courses. Consequently, some aspects, such as nutrition counselling, are neglected.

Insights from Survey Data on Training and Capacity

Health care provider survey data on training issues also support the results from the in-depth interviews on training received by the frontline workers (table 2.5). Approximately 48 percent of frontline workers reported that they had received some kind of nutrition training, including Basic Nutrition Training. Only 15 percent of health care providers had received Basic Nutrition Training from NNS. More than twice as many (32.8 percent) reported that they had received other nutrition training, but not the Basic Nutrition Training from NNS. More than half (52.1 percent) of health workers had not received any nutrition training. Note that the service providers who were interviewed were providers at the upazila health complexes (UHCs) and other facilities and are expected to get NNS training.

However, the training information from the research team's facility assessment showed that in 44 facilities across 6 districts, 28 percent of medical doctors, 35 percent of nurses, and 50 percent of CHCP had received Basic Nutrition Training (table A.6 and table A.7). The research team's assessment also showed that 28 percent of medical doctors and 32 percent of nurses had received IYCF training. Basic Nutrition Training coverage was found to be substantially low among sub-assistant community medical officers (SACMOs). The FWVs and IYCF training gap was predominant among SACMOs, FWVs, and CHCPs. Analysis of training coverage by facility type showed that overall nutrition-related training coverage was lower in union and community-level health facilities.

Table 2.7 presents the sources of nutrition training that the health care providers had gotten. IPHN is the leading source of Basic Nutrition Training as well as any nutrition training that the health care providers had attended. Very few health care providers reported that they had attended Basic Nutrition Training or any other nutrition training organized by IMCI and NGOs. In fact, very few health care providers who are responsible for service delivery at antenatal care/postnatal care (ANC/PNC) clinics (table A.6) and IMCI+Nutrition Corners (table A.7) received training in either NNS basic nutrition or IYCF at different levels of health facilities.

Table 2.7 Number of Health Care Providers Receiving Different Types of Nutrition Training from All Sources

Type of training received	MO (N = 26)	Nurse (N = 21)	FWV (N = 18)	SACMO (N = 38)	CHCP (N = 11)	FWA (N = 5)	Total (N = 119)
Received NNS Basic Nutrition Training	1	2	4	7	3	1	18
Received nutrition training (but not NNS Basic Nutrition Training)	8	7	6	11	4	3	39
Received no nutrition training	17	12	8	20	4	1	62

Note: Additional analysis of the data in table 2.5 will focus on identifying training status of NNS focal points within the upazila health complexes, especially those who are expected to train and orient other staff. CHCP = community health care provider; FWA = family welfare assistant; FWV = family welfare volunteer; MO = medical officer; NNS = National Nutrition Services; SACMO = subassistant community medical officer.

Table 2.8 Healthcare Providers Who Received Nutrition Training from All Sources, by Year, Pre-2012–14

Type of training received	Before 2012 N (%)	2012 N (%)	2013 N (%)	2014 N (%)
Basic Nutrition Training (N = 18)	0 (0)	2 (11.1)	12 (66.7)	4 (22.2)
Any kind of nutrition training excluding Basic Nutrition Training (N = 39)	11 (28.2)	2 (5.1)	13 (33.3)	13 (33.3)

Table 2.9 Number of Health Care Providers Who Received Training from Different Training Institutes

Type of training received	IPHN N (%)	IMCI section N (%)	NGO N (%)	Director of hospitals and clinics N (%)	Others N (%)	Do not know/cannot remember N (%)
Basic Nutrition Training (N = 18)	6 (33.3)	0 (0)	2 (11.1)	0 (0)	4 (22.2)	6 (33.3)
Any kind of nutrition training excluding Basic Nutrition Training (N = 39)	18 (46.2)	3 (7.7)	2 (5.1)	1 (2.6)	5 (12.8)	10 (25.6)

Note: IMCI = Integrated Management of Childhood Illnesses; IPHN = Institute for Public Health and Nutrition; NGO = nongovernmental organization.

Table 2.8 presents the number of health care providers who received nutrition-related training by the year the training was received. The number of health care providers who attended NNS Basic Nutrition Training was very low in all the years. However, a higher number of health care providers received some nutrition training other than NNS Basic Nutrition Training in every year. However, the number of health care providers who received general nutrition training, from NNS or any other sources, seems low compared to the number of health care providers at different levels of health facilities (table 2.9).

Summary of Findings on Training and Implementation Roll-Out

The operational assessment and interviews at the national level indicate that NNS training is getting underway after delays in the first year. However, record keeping of the training is inadequate. This inadequacy makes it difficult to assess exactly which types of training and support activities were completed in each upazila and how many people at which levels and positions were trained.

From a training design perspective, materials that were reviewed by the research team indicated dense training manuals with limited instructions for facilitators. These materials and the linked training package often required more time to get through than allocated for the training. If NNS intervention package is streamlined and prioritized, the training manuals could be revised accordingly. Several high-quality development partner training experiences exist in Bangladesh. Supporting training quality and implementation is a key area in which development partners could support NNS.

Other training challenges included the fact that a large number of front-line health staff received training for a variety of other government programs and also from NGOs and large projects. This diversity of training sources made the identification and branding of NNS training quite difficult. Survey data indicated very low coverage of NNS training (18 of 119) among NNS target workers in the upazila in which NNS had reported that training was been conducted. The monitoring of sources of training and extent of training of workers therefore was very challenging, but important to ensure efficiencies in training on similar topics for health professionals in an integrated health system.

Last, there are several ongoing problems with logistics and supplies for nutrition-related services. NNS now has initiated procurement of supplies through the Central Medical Stores Depot. Continued work is needed to streamline procurement processes with this depot.

Delivery of Services

Table 2.10 National Nutrition Services implementation and Service Delivery

Key research questions on service delivery	Research methods
• What is the overall *fidelity* to planned implementation and *quality* of service delivery of each of NNS interventions by health workers at different levels? Specifically: – Are good nutritional practices being promoted through nutrition education during facility-based service contacts (MO/SACMO/MA/ Nurses/FWV) and during community-based nutrition activities? – Are regular weight and height measurements of children 0–59 months during facility-based service contacts (MO/SACMO/MA/nurses/FWV) and during community-based nutrition activities (FWA, HA, CHCP) happening? – Do service providers know how to utilize the information they gain from GMP to address the specific issues being experienced by an individual child? – Is distribution of micronutrients to different target groups in place at different levels of service delivery system? – To what extent are the diagnoses and treatment of SAM/MAM by the service providers as per guidelines at all facilities and community level happening? Is a structured referral system working?	• Service provider surveys • Facility assessments (record review) • Structured observations • Focus group discussions with service providers • In-depth interviews with national stakeholders and service providers

Note: CHCP = community health care provider; FWA = family welfare assistant; FWV = family welfare volunteer; GMP = growth monitoring and promotion; HA = health assistant; MA = medical assistant; MAM = management of acute malnutrition MO = medical officer; NNS = National Nutrition Services; SACMO = subassistant community medical officer; SAM = severe acute malnutrition.

Box 2.3   What's Working Well in Implementation and Service Delivery?

Upgrading IMCI Treatment Corners to IMCI-Nutrition Corners Well Underway
- All facilities observed as part of the assessment included IMCI-Nutrition Corners.
- IMCI protocols already include guidance on specific nutrition-related activities (checking on feeding, assessing weights). However, the Basic Nutrition Training adds some value to screening SAM and MAM, elaborates on nutrition knowledge, and includes more detail on IYCF training.
- Both IMCI- and NNS-trained providers appear to offer more nutritional advice during sick child care.

Fairly Strong Nutrition Focus in ANC Service Delivery
- ANC case observations identified that providers do include several nutrition-specific actions in the ANC provision, including provision of iron-folic acid and some nutrition advice.
- All facilities visited included iron-folic acid supplementation as a core component in ANC.

Insights on National Nutrition Services Delivery from National-Level Stakeholders

National-level stakeholders raised a variety of issues related to NNS delivery. These issues included frontline worker workloads, incentives and motivations for service delivery across NNS delivery platforms, and strengthening outreach and demand for services.

Frontline Worker Workloads

Twelve of the 17 national-level interviews (which include NNS core team members) mentioned the problem of high frontline worker workloads as a challenge to integrate nutrition services into the existing government infrastructure. All categories of national-level interviewees were concerned about this issue.

Some interviewees suggested that creating a distinct cadre of frontline nutrition workers would help to reduce this pressure and prevent specific nutrition services from being neglected. However, such a step might not lead to an effective "mainstreaming" process unless such nutrition workers or counsellors were fully integrated into the health facilities/health system. District hospitals and upazila health complexes often are under great pressure to deal with urgent cases. As a result, the more preventive types of nutrition counselling and other nutrition services can suffer. Medical staff often are pressured to see large numbers of patients; so there often is very limited time at the IMCI+Nutrition Corners in these facilities to give nutrition advice or monitor patients.

Most interviewees considered that there was much more scope to do nutrition counseling in more primary-level facilities such as the community clinics (CCs). Even so, frontline workers such as HAs, FWVs, FWAs, and CHCPs also have heavy workloads. Moreover, because HAs and FWAs now devote three days per week at community clinics, these workers also have limited time to reach the large number of households in their areas with prevention and counselling.

Frontline Staff: Incentives, Motivation, and Staff Numbers

The national-level interviews also emphasized the incentives and motivation of frontline staff. These were seen as linked to training and supervision of these workers and to staff numbers. The interviews also suggested that if NNS managers visited facilities outside Dhaka more often, frontline workers would be more encouraged to carry out the nutrition side of their work.

Community-Based Mechanisms for Creating Awareness and Demand for Nutrition Services

Approximately seven of the interviewees drew attention to the need to create awareness and demand for nutrition services—especially through the community clinics. Community groups and community support groups attached to each community clinic could play an important role in creating awareness and demand in the clinics. Part of NNS's awareness-raising role through behavior change communication (BCC) should be to help these groups create demand, so that frontline service providers are approached more frequently for nutrition help and advice.

Insights on NNS Delivery from Subnational-Level Stakeholders and Unstructured Observations

Subnational interviewees raised a variety of issues related to NNS. Their perceptions centered around issues of coordination between the DGHS and DGFP actors, retention and motivation of providers, confusion and knowledge about NNS among providers, and availability of services and job aids.

Coordination across the DGHS–DGFP divide

Most of the field-level staff appeared able to collaborate across the DGHS–DGFP divide, especially within the community clinics. HAs and FWAs both worked in community clinics for three days each on different days and usually communicated well together. Nevertheless, sometimes cross-cutting issues such as nutrition were neglected because of a lack of clarity on which nutrition activities and messages these three categories workers were responsible for providing. The Comprehensive Training Plan has nutrition-related job descriptions for all relevant health service providers. However, the research team's interview findings suggest that the subnational- and field-level health care providers are not yet fully aware of their job descriptions with respect to nutrition services.

Most frontline workers mentioned that they tended to talk to clients about nutrition only when a specific problem arose, such as when breastfeeding or other feeding difficulties were presented to them. Apart from such incidents, their preventive advice tended to be very basic and general.

In the upazila health complexes and upazila family planning offices, there was more separation between the work of DGHS and DGFP staff than in the community clinics and family welfare centers. When upazila family planning offices were close to, or in the same building, as the upazila health complexes, proximity facilitated closer collaboration between DGHS and DGFP staff.

One upazila health and family planning officer (UHFPO) in Khulna district mentioned that even though, at the local level, DGHS and DGFP staff collaborated well in the field, in Dhaka, and sometimes at the upazila level, there was a tendency for DGHS and DGFP administrators to arrange their own meetings and other activities separately. This tendency undermined the two directorates' ability to collaborate effectively in the field in cross-cutting activities such as nutrition.

Problem of retention of medical officers

The senior staff interviewed had widespread concern about the impact of the lack of medical officers in upazila health complexes. These interviewees included MOs, residential medical officers (RMOs), UHFPOs, civil surgeons, and a district hospital superintendent. One issue was lack of recruitment. Another was that once MOs were recruited, they often managed to avoid being located at the upazila level through arranging alternative postings or training, usually in Dhaka. Staying out of the upazila level was considered to be the best way to progress in their careers. This belief is a widespread problem in Bangladesh. The result is a lack of medical staff at the upazila level, which means that remaining staff are under pressure to concentrate more on curative work and less on preventive work. The latter includes many of the nutrition services supported by NNS. In addition, even though MOs are receiving nutrition training in ToT courses, because they are less likely to settle in at the upazila level, they are not utilizing their training to train other frontline staff.

Moreover, many senior staff highlighted that, because of staff shortages, particularly in UHCs, MOs tended to concentrate their efforts on more urgent, curative cases. Again, the result was that the more preventive nutrition work was neglected. In the research team's qualitative observations, the IMCI+Nutrition Corners were functioning fully in all eight of the UHCs visited. Height and weight machines were being used. However, the growth monitoring charts did not seem to be in use. One upazila had no UHC. Two had UHCs, but their IMCI+Nutrition Corners were not functioning. Overall, in all the functioning IMCI+Nutrition Corners, the most time was spent treating large numbers of urgent cases rather than providing more preventive nutrition counselling.

Confusion and Limited Knowledge about Specific NNS and Links with Existing Platforms

Based on subnational interviews, most of the frontline interviewees were not sure which services were associated with NNS. Most were aware that the program had changed and that the *Pushti* packets (*Pushti apa*) and NGO nutrition activities had changed, but these interviewees did not know what had replaced them. Most of the senior management staff (civil surgeons, UHFPOs, and approximately half of the MOs) knew about NNS activities. One UHFPO and one FPO did not know about NNS. However, staff (health inspector [HI], assistant health inspector [AHI], HA, FWV, FWA, SACMO, CHCP) below the senior management level did not know much about NNS.

Most of the frontline staff also were confused about behavior change communication (BCC). Almost all of these staff thought that BCC referred to their own behavior, such as how to approach patients and how to behave in the communities in which they worked rather than how to promote awareness of specific health or family planning-related behavior in communities. Some FWAs knew what BCC referred to—but in regard to family planning services rather than nutrition. Not one frontline interviewee knew about BCC regarding nutrition.

All of the frontline staff had heard about severe acute malnutrition (SAM) and MAM. Most of them had heard about SAM and MAM from IMCI training. However, when asked about forms of malnutrition and treatments, approximately only 50 percent of the frontline workers knew in detail about what to do. They did know about giving nutrition advice and providing supplements. Two interviewees talked about providing ready-to-use therapeutic feeding.

Most of the interviewees reported that they rarely found SAM patients. In the few cases that they did find, they referred them to the UHC or to the district hospital. The district superintendent interviewee reported that if the district hospital could not properly manage a SAM patient–usually a child—the child would be sent to the nearest medical college hospital. One medical officer from Nilphamari reported that she sent SAM patients to a separate facility that had a child specialist.

Availability of National Nutrition Services, Equipment, and Job Aides

At community clinics, a range of nutrition-related supplies, including vitamins, iron-folic acid (IFA), and zinc, should be available. However, the research team found that, in reality, availability varied considerably. Calcium tablets were hardly available in any community clinic. Zinc treatment for diarrhea rarely was available. IFA usually was available. Vitamin A combined with deworming tablets usually was available when associated with the vitamin A+ national campaign. Vitamin B complex tablets sometimes were not available.

Findings on NNS Delivery from Facility Assessments, Case Observations, and Service Provider Interviews

The findings that follow draw from the quantitative data collected about NNS delivery. The findings address availability of services, quality of services provided, and extent to which nutrition interventions are integrated in the key NNS service delivery platforms.

Availability of NNS, Equipment, and Job Aides

Survey data show that IMCI+Nutrition Corners were functioning at all 12 (100 percent) upazila health complexes (table 2.11). As part of NNS program, the IMCI management corner at upazila health complexes have been strengthened to provide nutrition-specific interventions to children younger than five years of age. Hence, the service point is termed "IMCI+Nutrition Corner."

Distribution of IFA supplementation to pregnant women was in place in all 44 health facilities at district, upazila, and union levels. Distribution of Vitamin A supplementation during postnatal care (PNC) was found in 63.6 percent of the health facilities.

Table 2.11 Selected National Nutrition Services Implemented at Surveyed Health Facilities at Different Levels

Service	Number of facilities	Percent
Availability of IMCI+Nutrition Corner ($N = 12$)	12	100.0
IFA supplementation to pregnant women ($N = 44$)	44	100.0
Vitamin A supplementation during postnatal care ($N = 44$)	28	63.6

Note: IFA = iron-folic acid; IMCI = Integrated Management of Childhood Illnesses.

Table 2.12 Availability of Functioning Equipment, Logistics, and Job Aides at the Surveyed Health Facilities at District, Upazila, and Union Levels

Equipment, logistics, and job aides	District hospitals ($N = 6$)	Upazila health complex ($N = 12$)	Upazila health and family welfare centre ($N = 14$)	Community clinic ($N = 12$)	Total ($N = 44$)
Weighing scale	4	8	4	5	21
Height scale	2	7	4	3	16
Length scale	1	4	2	2	9
MUAC tape	2	4	3	6	15
GMP card (both girls and boys)	3	7	0	3	13
Register and reporting form	5	9	6	4	24
IMCI chart booklet	4	7	4	2	17
Module on basic nutrition	2	3	0	1	6
Guidelines for management of SAM/MAM	1	1	2	0	4
Guideline on community-based management of acute malnutrition	0	1	1	0	2
IYCF manual	1	2	0	0	3
Guideline on distribution of Vitamin A	2	4	1	1	8
Guideline on distribution of tablets and syrup for deworming	3	2	1	0	6
Referral slip	3	10	2	3	18

Note: GMP = growth monitoring and promotion; IMCI = Integrated Management of Childhood Illnesses; IYCF = infant and young child feeding; MAM = management of acute malnutrition; MUAC = mid-upper arm circumference; SAM = severe acute malnutrition.

Of 44 facilities assessed, only 21 (50 percent) had functioning weighing scales, and only 16 (36 percent) had a functioning height scale (table 2.12). Only 34 percent of facilities were found to use MUAC tape to identify severe wasting. Very few facilities had IMCI guidelines (38.6 percent), IYCF manuals (6.8 percent), or guidelines for SAM/MAM management (9.1 percent). Results for the availability of functioning equipment, logistics, and job aids at ANC/PNC and inpatient wards of the surveyed health facilities at district, upazila, and union levels are provided in table 2.12.

Infant and Young Child Feeding
Observation of the assessment of sick children at IMCI+Nutrition Corners revealed that only 1 in every 5 children less than 24 months of age was assessed for feeding practices (table 2.13). Regarding breastfeeding and complementary feeding, only 43.9 percent and 17.7 percent of caregivers of children less than 24 months of age were asked about breastfeeding and complementary feeding, respectively. Only 10 percent of caregivers were asked about changing feeding practices during an illness. SACMOs are the most commonly used providers for illness management of children younger than five years of age. However, NNS Comprehensive Training Plan does not currently include SACMOs as a target recipient of the Basic Nutrition Training (table A.10). Consequently, coverage of both Basic Nutrition Training and IYCF training was low among SACMOs (table A.6), even though they are among the most common care providers for illness management at the upazila health facilities.

Twenty-three percent of children presented with diarrhea. However, only 12 percent of caregivers of these children were advised on continued breastfeeding during diarrhea, and only 15 percent of these caregivers were counselled about the need to give more liquid or breast milk at home. Moreover, only 20 percent of the caregivers reported in exit interviews that they had received advice on providing oral rehydration solution to their children with diarrheal illness (data not shown). Zinc tablets were prescribed or provided by the health care providers to only 39 percent of children with diarrhea. Health care providers with IMCI training, Basic Nutrition Training, or both were more likely to provide advice on feeding practice (table 2.13).

Anthropometry and Identification of Severe Wasting, SAM/MAM
Observation of service delivery at IMCI+Nutrition Corners/illness management of children younger than five years of age revealed that only 20 percent of children who had attended the facilities had been weighed, and almost none had had a height or length measurement taken (table 2.13). Only 1 percent of the 0–59-month-old sick children were assessed for three of the following five danger signs: unable to drink or breastfeed; vomits everything; has had convulsions (more than one or prolonged >15 min); lethargic or unconscious; convulsing now (table 2.13). Having IMCI training or Basic Nutrition Training or both appears to increase the probability that the health care providers will measure the child's

Table 2.13 Observation of Illness Management of Children Less Than 5 Years of Age at IMCI+Nutrition Corners in Upazila Health Facilities

Observation points	No. of children eligible for service	No. of children who received service	Percent
Child checked for three danger signs[a]	842	5	0.6
Child checked for cough, diarrhea, and fever	842	153	18.2
Child less than two years of age assessed for feeding practices	504	28	5.6
Child weight measured and recorded	842	166	19.7
Child height/length measured and recorded	842	4	0.5
Child checked for visible severe wasting	842	6	0.7
Child's weight checked against a growth chart	842	43	5.1
Child checked if given anti-helminth (for children >1 year)	543	71	13.1
Health worker asked about breastfeeding (children >2 years)	504	221	43.9
Health worker asked about child taking other foods/fluids (for children >6 months)	711	126	17.7
Health worker asked about feeding change during illness	842	83	9.9
Health worker provided zinc tablet (for children with diarrhea)	194	76	39.2
Health worker explained the need to give more liquid or breast milk at home (for children with diarrhea)	194	29	15.0
Health worker explained the need to continue feeding or breastfeeding at home (for children with diarrhea)	194	23	11.9
Health worker advised on frequency of feeding	842	71	8.4
Health worker used mother's card/any visual job aid to demonstrate IYCF practices (for children 6–24 months)	373	5	1.3
Health worker counselled mothers on food and care required for under-weight children	—[b]	54	—
Health worker screened the child for SAM	842	43	5.1
Health worker counselled on ensuring one blue vitamin capsule for all children aged 6–11 months and 1 red Vitamin A capsule for all children aged 12–60 months	711	3	0.4
Health worker provided age-specific advice on inclusion of salt in all complementary food for children (for children aged more than 6 months)	711	2	0.3
Health worker prescribed/provided Vitamin A capsule (for children aged more than 6 months)	711	2	0.3
Health worker prescribed/provided tablet/syrup for deworming (for children aged more than a year)	543	10	1.9

Note: In subsequent analyses, the research team will examine service delivery by IMCI versus NNS training.
a. IMCI-specific indicator.
b. Number of children eligible for this service could not be identified because HCPs do not weigh the children while managing cases.

weight. However, height measurement was rare and not affected by training status. In exit interviews, 64 percent of caregivers reported that they had not received any feedback after a child's weight was measured (table 2.15), suggesting that the weight measurements were not being linked to even basic provision of information. Provision of feedback after weights were taken was better in upazila health complexes than in other facilities.

Child weights were plotted on the growth monitoring and promotion (GMP) cards for only 23 percent of cases (39 of 166) who were weighed (table 2.14).

Table 2.14 Nutrition Services during Illness Management of Children under Five by Age of Children, Sex, Type of Facility, Type of Health Care Providers, and Training of Health Care Providers

	Total	Child checked for three danger signs	Weight measured	Height/length measured	GMP card used	Screened for SAM	Feeding practice assessed from caregiver	Counselling on food and care given to mother	Prescribed nutritional supplements (ORS/zinc/Vit-A/salt inclusion) appropriate to illness/nutritional status of child
Total	842	1(5)	20(166)	0.5(4)	5(43)	5(43)	34(286)	6(54)	19(158)
Age of child (months)									
0–11	30(251)	2(4)	28(70)	0.8(2)	6(16)	7(17)	60(152)	7(18)	21(53)
12–23	21(176)	1(1)	19(33)	0	6(10)	3(6)	42(74)	7(13)	18(31)
24–35	18(152)	0	13(19)	0.7(1)	6(9)	5(7)	22(34)	9(13)	18(28)
36–47	15(129)	0	15(19)	0.8(1)	3(4)	5(7)	10(14)	2(3)	18(23)
48–60	15(128)	0	18(23)	0	3(4)	4(5)	7(9)	5(7)	18(23)
Sex of child									
Male	55(464)	1(3)	22(100)	0.2(1)	5(21)	5(25)	34(157)	7(35)	19(88)
Female	45(377)	1(2)	17(65)	0.8(3)	6(22)	5(18)	34(129)	5(18)	18(69)
Type of health facility									
UHC	79(663)	1(3)	24(157)	0.4(3)	6(40)	5(36)	39(259)	6(43)	21(138)
UHFWC	13(112)	0	5(6)	0.9(1)	2(2)	6(7)	15(17)	7(8)	11(12)
CC	8(66)	3(2)	5(3)	0	1(1)	0	15(10)	4(3)	12(8)
Type of HCP									
MO	3(29)	0	72(21)	0	10(3)	17(5)	48(14)	17(5)	27(8)
Nurse	2(16)	0	75(12)	0	6(1)	0	56(9)	25(4)	6(1)
FWV	7(58)	0	5(3)	1.7(1)	2(1)	5(3)	10(6)	2(1)	5(3)
SACMO	71(599)	1(3)	21(127)	0.5(3)	6(37)	6(34)	31(186)	7(41)	20(121)
CHCP	5(47)	2(1)	4(2)	0	2(1)	0	19(9)	6(3)	11(5)
Other (specify)	11(93)	1(1)	1(1)	0	0	1(1)	68(63)	0	21(20)
Training status of HCP		0.307	0	0.338	0	0.054	0.001	0	0.773
None	32(273)	0.4(1)	4(12)	1.1(3)	2(7)	3(8)	35(96)	4(12)	17(46)
IMCI trained	59(502)	0.6(3)	22(109)	0.2(1)	3(14)	7(34)	31(156)	5(25)	20(99)
NNS Trained	4(33)	0	48(16)	0	24(8)	0	39(13)	22(7)	21(7)
Both	4(34)	3(1)	85(29)	0	41(14)	3(1)	64(22)	29(10)	18(6)

Note: CC = community clinic; CHCP = community health care provider; FWV = family welfare volunteer; GMP = growth monitoring and promotion; IMCI = Integrated Management of Childhood Illnesses; MO = medical officer; NNS = National Nutrition Services; SACMO = subassistant community medical officer; UHC = upazila health complex; UHFWC = upazila health and family welfare centre.

The GMP card was more likely to be filled in UHCs than in other facilities (FWCs, CCs) (table 2.12). Having supplies of GMP cards could be critical since supplies of the GMP card were substantially lower in UHFWCs and CCs than in

UHCs (table 2.12). Only 3 percent of caregivers reported that service providers had showed them the child's weight on a growth monitoring chart. Children less than one year of age were more likely to be assessed for current feeding practice than other age groups.

In total, during the study period, 43 cases of SAM were detected at the IMCI+Nutrition Corners; of these, 36 (84 percent) were at the UHCs. Almost 50 percent of the identified SAM cases were admitted to the inpatient facilities; the remaining were provided with advice. Only 2 of 43 cases were referred to another facility. Screening children younger than five years of age for SAM was done primarily by medical doctors (that is, medical officers, or MOs) (table 2.14). Field enumerators observed that SAM was identified primarily through clinical assessments rather than through the use of weight and height measurements or other screening methods, such as MUAC tapes.

Overall, the assessment of sick-child care suggests that several missed opportunities exist for basic nutrition assessments and counselling, or at least reinforcement of messages about nutrition, during the sick-child visit. IMCI protocols, which already include some of these steps, clearly are not being fully adhered to, because either of case loads and lack of time or a general lack of attention and motivation to ensure a fully integrated management of each sick child.

Exit interviews of the caregivers of sick children younger than five years of age who sought care from the surveyed public health facilities revealed that the mean distance travelled by caregivers was 4.1 kilometer, and the mean travel time was 27 minutes (table 2.15). Across all types of facilities, fever, difficult breathing, and diarrhea of the child were the key reasons that caregivers reported for coming to the facility. Overall, 86 percent of the caregivers were satisfied with the service they had received from the public health facilities. Satisfaction level was particularly high in community clinics (95 percent).

Quality of Service Delivery at ANC Sessions

Observation revealed that 93.7 percent of pregnant women at the ANC sessions were weighed, and their weight was recorded (table 2.16). More than three-fourths (77.5 percent) of pregnant women were assessed for anemia status by looking at their eyes. More than a half (54.6 percent) of women with edema in the legs were examined at an ANC session. However, only 38.4 percent of women were measured and had their height recorded. Mothers were more likely to have had heights and weights measured and a physical examination conducted if the ANC service was provided by doctors or at UHCs (table 2.17). In fact, the research team noted that most (43 percent) of the ANC at UHCs was done by doctors, which explained the observed pattern. The proportion of women who received anthropometric measurements and physical examinations did not vary by maternal age but was higher among the pregnant women receiving their second or later ANC.

Advice provided by health care providers during ANC is shown in table 2.17. At ANC sessions, approximately two-thirds of pregnant women were given

Table 2.15 Distance and Time Travelled, Reason for Coming to the Facility, Feedback to Caregivers after Measuring Weight, and Showing Weight by Type of Provider

Type of facility	Upazila health complex	Upazila health and family welfare centre	Community clinic	Total
Travel distance (km; mean = 4, median = 2)				
Up to 1	32 (197)	79 (97)	74 (48)	42 (342)
1 to <2	21 (133)	14 (17)	14 (9)	20 (159)
2 to <3	14 (87)	3 (4)	3 (2)	11 (93)
3 & above	33 (209)	4 (5)	9 (6)	27 (220)
Travel time (mins; mean = 27, median =15)				
Up to 30	74 (462)	98 (121)	92 (60)	79 (643)
31 to 60	20 (123)	2 (2)	6 (4)	16 (129)
61 to 90	3 (17)	0	0	2 (17)
91 and up	4 (24)	0	2 (1)	3 (25)
Reasons for coming to facility				
Diarrhea	18 (109)	24 (28)	10 (6)	18 (143)
Vomiting	7 (42)	2 (2)	3 (2)	6 (46)
Fever/malaria	40 (245)	34 (40)	44 (27)	39 (312)
Difficult breathing/pneumonia	28 (175)	24 (29)	21 (13)	27 (217)
Ear problem	2 (15)	3 (3)	2 (1)	2 (19)
Well-child visit	0.2(1)	0	0	0.1 (1)
Others	51 (317)	47 (56)	68 (42)	52(415)
Feedback to caregivers after measuring the weight				
Mentioned weight	13(13)	0	0	13(13)
Said baby is growing well	14(14)	50(2)	0	15(16)
Said baby is not growing well	9(9)	0	0	9(9)
Didn't say anything to caregiver	64(63)	50(2)	100(1)	64(66)
Showed weight on growth monitoring chart	3(16)	0	0	0
Caregiver satisfied with service				
Very satisfied	4 (27)	16 (20)	3 (2)	6 (49)
Satisfied	87 (545)	78 (96)	95 (62)	86 (703)
Unsatisfied	7 (45)	6 (7)	2 (1)	7 (53)
Very unsatisfied	2 (10)	0	0	1 (10)

Note: UHFWC = upazila health and family welfare centre.

Table 2.16 Tasks Performed by Health Care Providers during Antenatal Care Case Management

Observation point	Upazila health complex (N = 339)	Upazila health and family welfare centre (N = 33)	Community clinic (N = 10)	Total (N = 382)
Weighed and recorded weight	322	27	9	358
Measured and recorded height	139	3	5	147
Examined anemia in eyes	267	20	10	297
Examined edema in leg	192	14	3	209

Note: UHFWC = upazila health and family welfare centre.

Table 2.17 Nutrition Services during Antenatal Care by Maternal Age, Gestational Age, Number of Antenatal Care Visits, Place, Type of Health Care Provider, Training of Health Care Provider

	Total	Anthropometric measurement (height and weight) taken	Adequate physical examination completed	Anemia assessed	IFA tablet given	Nutritional/ dietary advice given	Advice on breastfeeding given	Informed of essential newborn care practices	Notified of danger signs of pregnancy
		% (N)	% (N)	% (N)	% (N)	% (N)	% (N)	% (N)	% (N)
Total Mother's age	383	38 (146)	34 (131)	78 (297)	88 (333)	29 (110)	30 (115)	30 (114)	29 (112)
15–19	22 (86)	43 (37)	34 (29)	82 (71)	88 (76)	30 (26)	31 (27)	31 (27)	30 (26)
20–24	36 (138)	33 (46)	30 (42)	78 (108)	85 (118)	26 (36)	27 (38)	27 (37)	26 (36)
25–29	29 (111)	42 (47)	40 (44)	76 (85)	91 (99)	30 (33)	31 (35)	31 (35)	31 (35)
30–34	11 (43)	32 (14)	32 (14)	70 (30)	81 (35)	30 (13)	30 (13)	30 (13)	30 (13)
35–49	1 (5)	40 (2)	40 (2)	60 (3)	100 (5)	40 (2)	40 (2)	40 (2)	40 (2)
Gestational age									
1–12 weeks	9 (33)	18 (6)	15 (5)	79 (26)	94 (31)	15 (5)	15 (5)	15 (5)	15 (5)
13–26 weeks	42 (161)	45 (73)	42 (68)	81 (130)	93 (150)	36 (58)	40 (64)	40 (64)	38 (62)
>27	49 (189)	35 (67)	31 (58)	75 (141)	81 (152)	25 (47)	24 (46)	24 (45)	24 (45)
No. of ANC visit									
1	51 (197)	32 (64)	29 (57)	84 (165)	89 (176)	26 (52)	27 (53)	26 (52)	26 (52)
2–3	48.6 (186)	44 (82)	40 (74)	71 (132)	86 (157)	31 (58)	33 (62)	33 (62)	32 (60)
Type of health facility									
UHC	89 (339)	40 (138)	38 (129)	79 (267)	89 (299)	32 (109)	34 (115)	33 (114)	33 (112)
UHFWC	9 (33)	9 (3)	6 (2)	58 (19)	73 (24)	3 (1)	0	0	0
CC	3 (10)	50 (5)	0	100 (10)	100 (10)	0	0	0	0
Type of HCP									
MO	38 (146)	81 (119)	79 (115)	91 (133)	93 (133)	67 (99)	77 (112)	77 (112)	75 (110)
Nurse	3 (11)	9 (1)	9 (1)	36 (4)	18 (2)	9 (1)	9 (1)	9 (1)	9 (1)
FWV	13 (51)	23 (12)	4 (2)	72 (37)	80 (41)	12 (6)	0	0	0
SACMO	34 (131)	5 (7)	0	65 (85)	91 (119)	1 (2)	1 (1)	0	0
CHCP	2 (7)	43 (3)	0	100 (7)	100 (7)	0	0	0	0
Other	9 (35)	8 (3)	34 (12)	83 (29)	86 (30)	3 (1)	0	0	0
Training status of HCP									
None	79 (304)	45 (138)	39 (120)	84 (254)	88 (267)	36 (110)	38 (115)	37 (114)	37 (112)
Only NNS	14 (53)	6 (3)	0	43 (23)	81 (43)	0	0	0	0
Only EmOC	5 (21)	14 (3)	48 (10)	76 (16)	90 (19)	0	0	0	0
Both	1.3 (5)	40 (2)	20 (1)	80 (4)	100 (5)	0	0	0	0

Note: ANC = antenatal care; CHCP = community health care provider; EmOC = emergency obstetrics care; FWV = family welfare volunteer; HCP = health care provider. IFA = iron-folic acid; MO = medical officer; NNS = National Nutrition Services; SACMO = subassistant community medical officer; UHC = upazila health complex; UHFWC = upazila health and family welfare centre.

general advice to consume more foods with green leafy vegetables and to drink more water during pregnancy. Only one-third (33.4 percent) were advised to take iodized salt. Approximately 78 percent of pregnant women were advised to take IFA tablets during pregnancy.

However, advice related to infant and young child feeding (IYCF) appeared low. Only 34.5 percent of women were told about the importance of breastfeeding during childhood, and only 30 percent were told to initiate breastfeeding within an hour of the birth. Only 24 percent pregnant women were provided with messages on breastfeeding and on essential newborn care practices during their ANC in the third trimester (table 2.17). Only 30 percent of pregnant women were told about the child's danger signs during the neonatal period (table 2.18), and 29 percent were told about the maternal danger signs during birth (table 2.17). Medical officers were more likely to conduct physical examinations during ANC and give nutritional advice than other types of health providers (nurses, SACMOs).

Table 2.19 presents results for women who received medicines and pictorial cards during their ANC visits. Approximately 87 percent of pregnant women were either prescribed or supplied with iron-folic acid tablets from the facility.

Table 2.18 Types of Advice Provided to Pregnant Women by Health Care Providers during Antenatal Care Case Management

Advice	Number of women receiving advice (N = 383)	Percent
To consume more food	251	65.5
To ensure a balanced diet	239	62.4
To consume seasonal/available foods	214	55.9
To consume green/colored vegetables	230	60.0
To drink more water	241	62.9
To take iodized salt	128	33.4
To rest at least for two hours a day during daytime	176	46.0
To maintain personal hygiene	150	39.2
To consume routine iron and folic acid	299	78.1
Importance of breast feeding	132	34.4
Initiation of breastfeeding within an hour after birth	115	30.0
Danger signs for neonate	115	30.0

Table 2.19 Number of Pregnant Women Given Medicines and Pictorial Cards

Medicine/card	Upazila health complex (N = 336)	UHFWC (N = 33)	Community clinic (N = 13)	Total (N = 382)
Iron folate tablet	299	24	10	333
Calcium tablet	291	6	9	306
Vitamins	269	9	3	281
Pictorial card	120	1	2	123

Note: UHFWC = upazila Health and Family Welfare Centre.

Bangladesh National Nutrition Services • http://dx.doi.org/10.1596/978-1-4648-0640-7

Table 2.20 Service Delivery/Utilization at Different Health Facilities (*N* = 44) in the Study Area as Reported in the Health Facility Records

	Jessore (N = 7)	Khulna (N = 7)	Netrokona (N = 9)	Nilphamari (N = 7)	Cox's Bazar (N = 6)	Moulavibazar/ Sunamganj (N = 8)
ANC visits in last month	3,112	1,219	520	752	3,765	714[a]
PNC visits in last month	608	155	96	189	3,232	419
IFA tablets distributed to pregnant mothers in last month	—	—	14,100	10,147	22,980	10,868
IFA tablets distributed in last month	41,855	19,200	20,970	11,910	44,600	17,660
SAM children managed in last month	14	—	14	1	64	8
MAM children managed in last month	15	—	47	0	4	0

Note: "In last month" means in the last month that the facilities were surveyed for this study. ANC = antenatal care; IFA = iron-folic acid; MAM = management of acute malnutrition; PNC = postnatal care; SAM = severe acute malnutrition; — = not available.
a. Sunamganj was chosen in Moulavibazar district because Juri upazila was found to have a poor health infrastructure and a poorly functioning health facility.

Approximately three-fourths of women were provided with calcium and vitamins at the ANC sessions. However, only 32 percent of mothers were given pictorial cards.

As part of the research team's facility assessment for this study, the team collected data from the record books of the studied health facilities. Table 2.20 presents the number of ANC and PNC visits in the last month in the surveyed districts. Table 2.20 also presents the number of total IFA tablets distributed in the last month, the number of IFA tablets distributed to pregnant women, and the number of SAM and MAM cases being managed. These numbers indicate that SAM treatment numbers in particular were low; and could reflect issues with identification, care provision, and lower rates.

Community Clinics and HAs/FWAs: What Potential for Extending Outreach?

At the field level, nearly all interviewees were very positive about the ability of community clinics to improve the availability of health and family planning services. This ability includes exposure to a range of nutrition-related services, such as provision of vitamins and supplements, some nutrition advice, and many of the other services included in NNS operational plan. In the research team's qualitative research in the community clinics, the team found that adolescent girls were given treatment and advice about, among others, menstrual problems, hygiene and sanitation, and anemia. They were being provided with IFA and Vitamin B complex. However, the exposure of adolescent girls overall was limited because only those with problems came to the community clinics, and even then, only those who had easy access.

Also reported was exposure to nutrition education through satellite clinics when family welfare assistants (FWAs) visited areas for ANC, PNC, and family planning advice. These latter occasions took place sometimes in community clinics and sometimes in people's homes. At the family welfare clinics (FWCs), there also was exposure to nutrition-related counselling for pregnant mothers and mothers with infants. However, the research team did observe that some community clinics were not open at the times they should have been (for example, in Nilphamari).

At the same time, some of the issues that arose through interviews or through observations by the research team raised the following findings on service delivery at the community clinics:

- Training and capacity of the CHCPs (who are the major service providers in CCs) is limited. Eight of 14 CHCPs and four of five FWAs interviewed by the subnational quantitative field team reported that they had not received Basic Nutrition Training from NNS.
- A core component of service delivery by the CHCPs is monitoring the weight and height of the children. Eleven of 12 CCs surveyed had functioning height and weight scales. However, the case observation results (see tables on community clinics in appendix B) indicate that only 3 of 66 children's weight was measured and recorded by the health care providers, while none of these children's height was measured and recorded. Only 1 of these 66 children's weight was checked against a growth chart. Only two were checked for the three danger signs.
- Of the 65 exit interviews of caregivers at the CCs, 40 reported that they thought the provider's prescription was good. None reported it as bad/very bad, indicating a good degree of satisfaction with service delivery.
- As described elsewhere, NNS suffers from a lack of staff to actively monitor field-level facilities, especially in CCs, which often are located in remote areas. This lack of monitoring, in turn, appeared to create a lack of motivation among frontline workers and the opportunity to skip their work without penalty. At the same time, 9 of 12 facilities surveyed had been visited by an external supervisor at least once in the previous six months. However, it is not clear whether the visit examined nutrition services as well or how often each facility had been visited. Once in six months could be considered low for a supervisory visit.
- The research team frequently experienced difficulties in finding CCs that were operating on the day of visit, even though visits were during operating hours. The team also noted that some CCs are housed in such shabby buildings that service delivery during extreme weather conditions stopped altogether. Only one in eight CCs visited had an electricity connection, the lack of which definitely is an obstacle against providing quality service.
- As with the upazila facilities, CCs are visited primarily by sick clients. Consequently, counselling messages delivered through CCs likely have very limited reach into the general population.

Box 2.4   Family Welfare Volunteers and Health Assistants: What Is Their Potential to Extend Outreach?

Family Welfare Volunteers (FWVs)

Activities:

- FWVs mainly work at FWC and also attend satellite clinics. They sometimes provide services directly at the UHC.
- Activities include registration of pregnant women and newlyweds; provision of ANC and PNC; provision of advice to pregnant women about having nutritious foods (fish, meat, eggs, lentils, green leafy vegetables, fruits), eating more food and drinking plenty of water, avoiding heavy work, and resting during pregnancy; advice to HH members on care of pregnant women and newborns; advice on child care and feeding (colostrum, exclusive breast feeding, continue breast milk for two years, complementary feeding from six months of age) and immunization; advice to adolescent girls and women about menstrual problems, and advice on family planning. FWCs also provide contraceptive pills, intrauterine devices (IUDs), and supplements including iron and folic acid tablets, Vitamin B complex, zinc for diarrhea, and itamin A to mothers after delivery.

Health Assistants (HAs)

- They work three days in a week in the community clinics, where they provide primary treatment and medicines to patients. They also refer patients to the upazila hospital if needed. They spend two days a week doing EPI activities in which they register new children for immunizations. On those days, they also provide health education to family members and patients. Another responsibility, one day a week, is to provide health education to the community through schools, madrasas, and Uthan Boithok.
- They also provide ANC and PNC services. Male HA only deliver messages. Female HAs often provide other more direct medical support to pregnant mothers.

Training, Capacity, and Motivation

- FWVs reported receiving basic training on family planning methods and some BCC training. Some also reported receiving IMCI training and nutrition training from an NGO (World Vision).
- FWVs felt that they are capable to do their job. They also felt that they had the capacity but needed proper logistics support and regular supplies, as well as extra staff support.
- FWVs noted that they have a tremendous workload and would like additional staff support to deliver services. They also noted that training could be motivating by increasing their knowledge, but also noted that the financial incentives for their family planning work are highly motivating.

- HAs reported a heavy workload and noted that they were unable to follow up patients often. They felt that they could provide basic treatment to most patients and that they had received basic training for their primary jobs. Some recalled received a six-day training on Vitamin A, anemia, iodine, and zinc, but noted that they did not really get any training on nutrition. They, therefore, felt limited in their ability to provide nutrition services.
- They felt pleased that the community was getting good information from them and also felt that society was changing for the better because of their work.

Box 2.4 outlines some of the team's findings regarding the possibility of engaging the HAs/FWVs in extending outreach, especially of preventive services. The research team's sample for this cadre of workers was limited. Nevertheless, the key insights appear to be that both the CC and the HA/FWV cadres offer some potential for extending outreach, of both preventive and curative care, but that there are some key hurdles along the way that need be addressed. These hurdles concern capacity, motivation, quality of CC facilities, and supervision/monitoring mechanisms.

All of the aforementioned issues are substantial challenges. However, a time-limited cadre of staff who are similar to HAs/FWVs might offer a way to experiment with truly mainstreaming quality preventive nutrition services and screening for SAM if a focused effort is made to explore and establish services through careful feasibility studies.

Summary of Findings on Service Delivery

In spite of the roll-out of the training, the research team's results study highlighted that many frontline health and family planning workers did not seem to fully understand how and why NNS had changed from the previous NNP program. It appears that much clearer communications and guidance is needed with these workers about how NNS functions, what has changed after NNP, why, what their responsibilities now are, and how these link with their existing positional responsibilities.

Service delivery under NNS is intended to occur through diverse delivery platforms: IMCI+Nutrition Corners, ANC, inpatient care, sick-child visits at community clinics, and outreach through HAs and FWVs. Each of these delivery platforms has its inherent challenges related to coverage, reach, quality, and utilization, as well as platform-specific challenges to integration of nutrition interventions. NNS interventions delivered through these platforms therefore also are subject to platform-specific basic challenges and nutrition integration challenges.

- *IMCI+Nutrition Corners.* IMCI protocols already include guidance on specific nutrition-related activities (such as checking on feeding, assessing weights). The research team's case observations of children brought into sick-child care offered at the IMCI indicate that this component is lagging behind the basic clinical diagnostic and prescriptive nature of sick-child care. However, given that some nutrition care already has been incorporated into basic IMCI protocols, emphasizing the nutrition activities as part of ongoing IMCI training can help strengthen this activity. Nevertheless, the issue remains that children coming into IMCI+Nutrition Corners in the health facilities are primarily sick children, and providers' focus tends to be on clinical care and case treatment. The ages of children in sick-child care also vary tremendously.

Therefore, targeting IYCF counselling in what is a hurried, illness-focused contact is fundamentally more challenging.

- *ANC.* As with IMCI, ANC protocols also appear to already include some nutrition focus. Our ANC case observations highlight that providers do include several nutrition-specific actions in the ANC provision. The reason could be that the ANC platform is fundamentally a prevention-focused platform and reaches directly the target of the nutrition interventions—the pregnant woman.
- *Referral and inpatient care for SAM.* According to the health facility assessment carried out by the research team, referrals for SAM are limited or inaccurate because providers are not investing in weighing and measuring the children who come into the IMCI+Nutrition Corners. In most facilities observed, the number of SAM children managed in the previous months usually was two or fewer. SAM cases need careful investigation. Referrals also should be followed up and appropriate treatment given in compliance with national guidelines.
- *Sick-child visits at community clinics.* Case observations of sick-child care reveals extremely poor performance related to weighing of sick children seen in the community clinics, in spite of a greater availability of equipment than IMCI+Nutrition Corners. Strengthening care protocols for sick children brought into the community clinics and ensuring logistics supply and monitoring and supervision of SAM/MAM screening could help to strengthen nutrition-focused service components, too.
- *Outreach through HAs/FWVs.* This study did not explicitly examine actual service delivery by HAs and FWVs. Observing outreach services is logistically highly challenging, and the study did not include a population-based survey to examine the extent to which households were visited by HAs/FWVs. Nevertheless, the qualitative interviews with these frontline staff revealed their almost complete lack of awareness or knowledge about nutrition-related services, including BCC and demand-creation for services at the community clinics. Exposure to NNS training was low as well. Clearly, a detailed assessment of training processes that relate to these frontline workers is essential, as is an assessment of what specific roles they are to play within NNS.

Overall, there is great variability in the integration of nutrition interventions and actions into these delivery platforms. Much remains to be done to truly integrate nutrition into these health services. Furthermore, given the current levels of use of these platforms, the eventual coverage of NNS interventions, even if delivered much better than now through these platforms, may never reach the levels necessary to impact the general population. Analysis of the Bangladesh Demographic and Health Survey (BDHS 2011) data showed that only 25 percent of mothers (with live births in the previous three years) had come in contact with a public health facility during their pregnancies for ANC. Twelve percent had delivered in a public facility. Only 11 percent had received postnatal care (PNC) at a public facility. The percentage of mothers in contact with a public facility for all three services (ANC, delivery, PNC) was very low (5.2 percent) (table 2.21). Therefore, even if all NNS interventions were available at all levels of public health facilities, they would reach only 25 percent of mothers during pregnancy and 5 percent of babies during the entire prenatal to postnatal period.

The sick-child management/IMCI platform, by definition, is accessed only by mothers/caregivers who have a sick child. Data from the 2011 BDHS show that only 25 percent–35 percent of children sick with diarrhea, acute respiratory infection, or fever were taken to a health facility or to a formal health care provider for treatment. These data confirm that the population coverage that potentially could be achieved through these platforms is quite limited.

Nevertheless, there are areas of better performance, for example, IMCI+Nutrition and ANC. However, clearly, deep challenges relating to service delivery and supervision exist for the community clinics and the outreach services by the HAs and FWAs. Training coverage among these service providers also is low. To the research team's knowledge, there was no piloting of specific NNS interventions within each of these platforms before implementing mainstreamed services at a larger scale. There also is no ongoing learning or review process in place to assess implementation challenges.

Therefore, the scope appears limited for learning approaches through implementing NNS via such diverse implementation modalities. *The key recommendation is that NNS consider integrating feasibility assessments, technical review missions, and other learning approaches to assess the delivery of at least a few prioritized critical interventions.* NNS, and its funders, should undertake a critical analysis to identify platforms (including NGO-based platforms) that will enable NNS to have the highest population impact. Developing a process for continuous learning that engages technical partners, first, can strengthen overall implementation plans. Second, building in continuous learning can provide NNS managers with the opportunity to learn more about on-the-ground implementation processes to ensure program fidelity.

Table 2.21 Mother–Newborn Pairs (N = 3,264) Who Had Contact with Public Health Facilities during the Prenatal, Delivery, and Postpartum Periods

Type of contact with public health facility	Percent
Had ANC contact	25.5
Had delivery	12.4
Had PNC contact	10.8
Had ANC contact and delivery	6.6
Had ANC and PNC contact	5.6
Had delivery and PNC contact	10.2
Had ANC, PNC contact, and delivery	5.2

Note: "Public health facility" includes government hospital, upazila health complex, family welfare clinic, satellite clinic, and community clinic. ANC = antenatal care; PNC = postnatal care.

Monitoring and Evaluation

Table 2.22 Monitoring and Evaluation

Key research questions on monitoring and evaluation	Research methods/sources
• What are the current arrangements for monitoring and evaluation of NNS interventions and how well is NNS monitoring integrated with the broader health system monitoring? • Are nutrition indicators included in the current health management information system (HMIS)? Which ones? Do they cover all key NNS interventions? • What are the available mechanisms to collect routine information on nutrition service contacts and anthropometric measurements?	• National-level in-depth interviews with NNS staff • Service provider surveys • Facility assessments (record review) • Focus group discussions with service providers • In-depth interviews with service providers

Note: HMIS = health management information system; NNS = National Nutrition Services.

Reporting System

As initially intended, the current monitoring system for NNS interventions is linked with the Routine Health Management Information Systems (RHMIS). At the time of writing, nutrition indicators for children younger than five years had been incorporated in the routine RHMIS through the monthly IMCI+Nutrition Corner reporting format and monthly community clinic reporting format for newborn and child health.

The research team's review of IMCI+Nutrition Corner Monthly Reports reveals that nutrition indicators have been incorporated in the reporting format. However, there are several limitations on what is included in this reporting format, including the choice of indicators.

- *Low birth weight (within 72 hours of birth)*. This information was very difficult to get from the IMCI+Nutrition Corner. Collecting this information based on recall may be biased. In addition, very few neonates with low birth weight are likely to come to the IMCI-Nutrition Corner outdoors within 72 hours of birth.
- *IYCF indicators (early initiation of breastfeeding, exclusive breastfeeding up to six months, and complementary feeding)*. Reporting these indicators from the IMCI Nutrition Corner will depend on the mother's recall of children younger than five years presented at the facility with any illness for the first time.
- *Stunting and wasting (0–5 years)*. Anthropometry training, including measurement of length/height, should be ensured for service providers because IMCI only measures weight-for-age. The existing growth monitoring chart does not have the weight-for-height curve to identify wasting.
- *ANC and PNC utilization*. No nutrition indicators have been incorporated in the reporting format for ANC and PNC use.

Box 2.5   What's Working Well with Monitoring?

Nutrition Information System
- There has been considerable progress in institutionalizing the reporting of nutrition indicators in the Routine Health Management Information Systems (RHMIS) through revisions to the monthly IMCI-Nutrition Corner reporting format and the monthly community clinic reporting format for newborn and child health.
- An MIS consultant is now in place at NNS, and information has started flowing into NNS Dhaka offices.

Program Performance Reviews
- Limited supervisory visits are taking place at the health facilities level.

In addition to these limitations on reporting, there were various service provider complaints regarding the registers and reports. The reports submitted by the upazila- and union-level health facilities often were incomplete. On the other hand, health facilities complained that including nutrition indicators with the IMCI report made reporting complicated and more difficult.

Perceptions of Monitoring

The NNS core team made it clear that monitoring mechanisms are in place but are implemented in different ways by the IMCI Nutrition Corners, the existing family planning mechanism, and the community clinics. Most of the interviewees emphasized the need for good monitoring. However, some non-NNS interviewees expressed frustration that not enough monitoring was being done, especially regarding whether what was included in nutrition training was being implemented by frontline staff.

Management Information: Indicators, Record-Keeping, Compilation, and Review

All four NNS core team members interviewed spoke positively about the recent progress in recording and use of management information about NNS progress. They mentioned not having nutrition indicators included in monitoring tools in the past, but said that these indicators slowly were being incorporated in management information collected at the various facilities. They also were aware that frontline health and family planning workers should not be overburdened with unnecessary record keeping.

At the same time, hardly any of the interviewees at the subnational level knew about any monitoring for nutrition activities. The only relevant record keeping was for ANC when a pregnant woman's details were recorded, and in the community clinics for medicine supplies and distribution. At the UHC, medicine records also were kept. The IMCI+Nutrition Corners were not keeping reliable records of patients because of time pressure.

Bangladesh National Nutrition Services • http://dx.doi.org/10.1596/978-1-4648-0640-7

Thus, for nutrition activities, there did not seem to be much evidence of the use of indicators, record keeping, or compilation or review of information at the field level. Moreover, apart from accounting purposes, we saw no evidence of record keeping, compilation, or review of training activities at the upazila level or below.

Field Visits and Communication between NNS in Dhaka and Upazila and Community Clinics

Field visits and communication between NNS in Dhaka and upazila and community clinics arose in more than half of the interviews. These were discussed negatively by development partners, who felt that NNS management staff were rarely visible at the field level as they should have been. This lack of field visitation was seen as limiting the ability of NNS staff to encourage frontline staff to implement the mainstreaming of nutrition services.

One development partner was surprised that

> …they asked us in Dhaka about how the training at the field level went. They were not able to go to the field themselves.

However, some of the interviewees felt that the heavy workloads and demands to attend meetings in Dhaka prevented them from going to the field as often as they should.

Some NNS core team members felt that they were not expected to visit field-level activities:

> The staff at field level are not under my payroll. I do not monitor them and neither am I their supervising authority. I sit in Dhaka and give them phase-by-phase training. We orient them through training and hope for their ownership of the program at the field level.

Other NNS core team members did think that field visits were expected of them, but felt doing so was not possible because they were tied up with desk-based and central-level work.

Survey data show that supervision as part of the capacity building of health care providers, particularly visits by external supervisors to the health facilities, is good in most surveyed districts, except in Jessore (table 2.23). In Khulna and Nilphamari districts, all six health facilities were visited at least once by an external supervisor, as opposed to Jessore, in which only one of six health facilities was visited by an external supervisor. The mean time for all districts combined since the last visit by an external supervisor was 1.1 ± 1.5 months; the median time (range) was 1 (0–6) month. It is not known how many of these external supervisors were from the Line Directorates for DGHS/DGFP versus from NNS itself.

Table 2.24 shows the activities observed by an external supervisor during the last visit to upazila health complexes, UHFWC, and community clinics. Observation of childhood illness management at IMCI+Nutrition Corners (100 percent) was very high, as opposed to observation of ANC sessions (63.6 percent) and SAM case management at inpatient (63.3 percent) service.

Table 2.23 Number of Health Facilities Visited by an External Supervisor at Least Once in the Last Six Months, by Districts Surveyed

District	No. of health facilities surveyed N = 44	No. of facilities visited by an external supervisor
Jessore	7	2
Khulna	7	7
Nilphamari	7	6
Netrokona	9	7
Cox's Bazar	6	4
Moulvibazar/Sunamgonj[a]	8	6

a. Moulvibazar and Sunamganj are presented together because only one upazila was surveyed from each of these two districts.

Table 2.24 Supervisory Visit by External Supervisors at Upazila Health Complex, Upazila Health and Family Welfare Centre, and Community Clinic

Activity observed by external supervisor during last visit	Number	Percent
ANC session (N = 44)	28	63.6
Childhood illness management at IMCI+Nutrition Corner (N = 12)	12	100.0
SAM management at inpatient (N = 11)	7	63.3

Note: ANC = antenatal care; IMCI = Integrated Management of Childhood Illnesses; SAM = severe acute malnutrition.

Summary of Findings and Recommendations Regarding Monitoring

The overall findings of the research team on monitoring to strengthen NNS performance are that three challenges could be substantial roadblocks to ensuring that program performance is on track.

1. *NNS record keeping for monitoring purposes seems weak.* The system of collection and transmission of information is poorly understood and poorly used. Information on implementation roll-out and development partner support to geographic and technical areas was hard to obtain or was unavailable. *Strengthening record keeping within NNS should be a primary focus at this stage of program implementation.* This is crucial to ensure that information on implementation roll-out, performance/outputs, and development partner support to geographic and technical areas is easily available to all key stakeholders and is routinely updated.
2. Despite the development of a set of nutrition indicators for mainstreaming in the health management information system, *there are challenges with some indicators such as stunting* (which are close to impossible to assess in a facility-based HMIS). In addition, there is a legitimate concern about overloading frontline workers with excessive record keeping.

Table 2.25 Exposure to National Nutrition Services Interventions

Key research question on exposure to NNS interventions	Data sources
What is the level of exposure to different NNS service delivery components among households who are potential users of NNS services?	Exit interviews Qualitative interviews with users of NNS services

Note: NNS = National Nutrition Services.

The research team recommends two changes:

a. A careful review of the current set of NNS indicators for inclusion in the HMIS

b. Prioritization of a few indicators that are indicative of extent and quality of service delivery, rather than of actual nutrition statistics, such as low birth weight or stunting.

3. *A system for technical monitoring of service quality by experts is largely absent.* NNS staff at the Dhaka level are too busy and do not make the needed field visits to examine program performance. Even though some supervisory visits are taking place at the level of the health facilities, it is not clear to the research team whether these visits aim to ascertain both basic service provision and nutrition intervention quality. Field supervisory visits are an area in which NNS can draw upon the capacity of development partners, who have both technical capacity and, in several cases, local field presence. Developing a streamlined technical visit and a web-based data input system for recording site visits could facilitate organized and systematic field supervision visits.

Findings from Exit Interviews on Service Delivery

Exit interviews with caregivers of children who came to seek health care at the IMCI+Nutrition Corners showed that approximately 18 percent of children had diarrhea (table A.9). Other reasons for visiting health facilities by children are provided in table A.9.

As reported by the caregivers in exit interviews, only 13.0 percent of the 816 children who had visited the facilities were weighed (table 2.26). Of the 36.2 percent of children who were measured, the health care providers told something to the caregivers after weighing the child in only 4.7 percent of the cases. Only 30.6 percent of caregivers reported that they had received any advice from

Table 2.26 National Nutrition Services Provided by the Health Care Providers, as Reported by the Caregivers

Services	Number	Percent
Child's weight was measured by health worker	105	13.0
Health worker told caregiver something after weight measurement	399	36.2
Health worker (doctor) told caregiver something about feeding	247	30.6
Caregiver asked health worker any question regarding feeding	65	8.0
Total	816	100.0

Table 2.27 Types of Health Care Providers Attending Sick Children, as Reported by Caregivers in Exit Interviews

Types of health care provider	Number of children (N = 811)	Percent
Medical officer	162	19.9
Nurse	1	0.1
Family welfare volunteer	61	7.5
Sub assistant community medical officer	527	64.9
Community health care provider	60	7.4

the health care providers on child feeding. A scant few caregivers (8.0 percent) had asked any questions of the health care providers regarding child feeding.

Table 2.27 presents the type of health care providers who had given services to children who went to the facilities seeking care. Approximately 20 percent of the children were seen by a medical officer. The highest number (65 percent) of sick children was managed by a SACMO. As health care providers to sick children, FWVs and CHCPs were low, both at 7.5 percent.

Summary of Findings on Exposure to NNS Interventions

This operational assessment focused on examining the state of implementation and service delivery of NNS interventions. Of these, the primary focus were the platforms and geographic areas that were the most ready for implementation assessment. As a result, and by design, this assessment did not include a population-based survey to assess usage rates and exposure to NNS delivery platforms.

Although most of the platforms assessed reached relatively fewer children, the research team noted that, even within these platforms, some opportunities were missed to deliver all relevant services to mothers/children who reached these service points. For example, the category of "any ANC use" was 68 percent of all pregnant women, but only 41 percent of that category was ANC provided in public sector facilities. Therefore, public sector facilities have at least one ANC contact with no more than 28 percent of pregnant women (BDHS 2011).

Similarly, since the IMCI platform is intended to reach primarily sick children, its reach is limited. However, the research team's findings indicate that strengthening IMCI itself at least can ensure that key nutrition interventions reach the vulnerable populations who are the most likely to be at risk of being severely malnourished and that there are no missed opportunities.

Data on usage rates for community clinics are not yet available, but here again, the research team's findings indicate that CCs are a platform that currently reach sick children for the most part.

Thus, until a platform is identified for NNS that is truly focused on reaching target populations *preventively*, some services, such as IYCF counselling, simply will not be delivered at scale. Using the health-focused outreach platforms and frontline workers, and experimenting with modalities such as specific preventive outreach days, preventive outreach workers, and other strategies to strengthen preventive outreach will be central to achieve coverage at scale.

Development Partner Support to NNS

The research team's in-depth interviews explicitly aimed to elicit information about development partner support to NNS. Some information on partner support was available in the initial national-level interviews. After the initial analysis, additional interviews were done with NNS to gather more information on the roles of key development partners in supporting NNS.

All NNS core team members talked positively about the supportive roles played by UNICEF, DFID, and Save the Children. UNICEF also was mentioned by other NNS platform, ministry, and policy-level interviewees as providing technical support, logistics, and training materials, as well as support to policy and strategic planning and event hosting. Finally, UNICEF is seen as providing support more in kind than in funding, but also is identified as providing constructive criticism to the NNS team. One NNS core team member said, "UNICEF works as a safety net for us." In addition to the central level, UNICEF has been providing support to NNS field-level implementation in different parts of the country, especially to BCC and SAM management. Box 2.6 highlights UNICEF's attempts to provide support to NNS and reports NNS and UNICEF staffs' reflections on the process and its outcomes.

The NNS core team members also noted that Save the Children was providing technical support through their Tackling Childhood Malnutrition (TCM) project, including hands-on training on using modules and addressing logistics issues. In fact, during a period when logistics supplies were not available from GoB, it was noted that Save the Children supplied NNS logistics inputs. It also was noted that Save the Children supported NNS reporting system in addition to support with service delivery and training, and provide some funding for those components that they are involved with. Save the Children has a focal person for monitoring in four upazila. Interviews with Save the Children confirmed this. One interviewee noted, "Our work is based on a problem solving approach, where we identify problems and challenges faced at the field level and address those there. Later provide feedback to the central level to help them address similar challenges in other areas." In addition to the four upazila with intensive and direct support, Save the Children also provides support to other 29 upazila.

The other development partner mentioned frequently was DFID, including that DFID provided NNS with two consultants to support work on human resources (HR) and M&E. The NNS core team members appreciated the support from the M&E consultant and noted that his technical inputs as well as his presence during bilateral meetings were beneficial. In contrast, some challenges were

Box 2.6 Example of Development Partner Support to NNS: UNICEF

Development partners in Bangladesh aim to provide diverse types of support to the Government of Bangladesh's health and nutrition programs to strengthen capacity and implementation. A recent report on the UNICEF Maternal and Child Nutrition Program describes and reflects on UNICEF's support to the Government of Bangladesh. The report describes UNICEF's support in mainstreaming "direct nutrition interventions" (DNIs) in existing health and family planning services. UNICEF's focus was nutrition-specific interventions such as IYCF and hygiene, micronutrient powder supplementation, deworming, consumption of nutrient-rich fortified foods, SAM management, and maternal nutrition.

Reported examples of UNICEF support were as follows:

- A national nutrition capacity assessment that led to the development of UNICEF District Nutrition Support Officers specifically to support multisectoral planning
- Support to IYCF national communications campaign
- Development of communications tools and job aids for growth monitoring and IFA
- Procurement of equipment and job aids for United Nations Development Assistance Plan (UNDAP) districts
- Support to supply planning and forecasting for supplies
- Support to monitoring by integrating nutrition indicators into HMIS and establishing a National Nutrition Information and Planning Unit within the Ministry of Health and Family Welfare (MoHFW)
- Development of a national protocol for SAM management.

The UNICEF report reflects on lessons learned through its providing support to the Government of Bangladesh for DNIs. UNICEF raises specific issues such as that challenges to utilization are major constraints against achieving IFA coverage and iodized salt. UNICEF includes service provision and utilization as challenges to improving complementary feeding. Perhaps more important, the UNICEF report also notes that improving the quality of direct nutrition interventions is crucial to reduce undernutrition in Bangladesh. They also note several challenges related to human resource capacity, definitions of indicators and targets for the nutrition interventions, and provision of area-based support to ensure demonstrable models for scale-up.

Other challenges were lower donor commitments to nutrition than needed, need for better evaluation of the kind of development partner support provided by UNICEF to the government (for example, the District Nutrition Support Officers), and a lack of community-level mechanisms for effective outreach.

In a critical timeframe such as 2014/15, during which the HPNSDP OP is being revised, it appears important to examine the insights from UNICEF's, and other (where available) development partners' and NGOs' support to the Government of Bangladesh's actions to scale up nutrition interventions through NNS.

Source: UNICEF Bangladesh 2014.

raised around the use of a consultant to support human resources issues: "HR issues should be handled from the Ministry. The consultant does not have much role to play here." For its part, DFID was positive about developments made in the NNS monitoring and information system (MIS), noting that, despite the long delay, DFID was finally receiving MIS data from the system.

The World Bank was mentioned specifically as the primary funding agency for NNS, and its inputs in policy and strategic support also were noted. One NNS core team member said, "They provide policy and strategic support. Through audit they were able to identify gaps in management areas of NNS."

Other development partners such as International Centre for Diarrhoeal Disease Research, Bangladesh (ICDDR, B), Helen Keller International, FHI360, A&T, or SPRING also were mentioned during interviews. However, it appears that none of these agencies had direct agreements with NNS to provide support. It was noted that some of these development partners also were contracted by other funders to accomplish specific tasks that would support NNS. Prior linkages with SPRING and the FANTA program also were mentioned. For these two, it was noted that earlier there had been good linkages with NNS but that, at present, the linkages were more limited.

> Overall, NNS was appreciative of the support from the key development partners. The development partners also had a generally affirmative view toward progress made by the NNS team with their challenging portfolio. Specifically, the partners recognized the hurdles that NNS faced but noted that progress was being made.

Analysis and Recommendations

Ensuring adequate development partner support to NNS is critical to ensure availability of funds, technical support for training and service delivery, monitoring support, and engaging in NNS-related research/learning. At the time of writing, no *systematic* documentation is available on the nature, extent, and diversity of development partner support to NNS. The interviews revealed a variety of types of support. Based on them, the research team recommends that a catalogue be developed of current development partner and other technical partner support to NNS. This catalogue should include information on technical areas that are being supported as well as service provision in local areas that is being supported. This catalogue would help greatly to map existing needs with available development partner support in ways that best benefit the Government of Bangladesh's program.

CHAPTER 3

Key Lessons and Recommendations

Abstract

Chapter 6 discusses the key insights and recommendations that emerged from this operational assessment of National Nutrition Service (NNS) in Bangladesh. The key lessons and recommendations are subsequently presented under five broad groups: program design, institutional issues and governance, training and roll-out, program implementation/service delivery, and monitoring and evaluation.

For service delivery especially, the data collected by the team came from a set of upazila identified as forerunners in receiving NNS training and other inputs. The expectation, therefore, is that these upazila also had somewhat more "settled" implementation. Their more mature program is not representative of the entire country. That these upazila are the best-case scenario should be noted when interpreting results.

Program Design

Regarding the design of the NNS program, two central issues emerged from this research. The first issue was the lack of specificity in choosing the number of interventions, which led to too many interventions to be coordinated and delivered by NNS. The second was the choice of delivery platforms for the core direct nutrition interventions (DNIs). Core issues that relate to the choice of platform for each DNI are summarized in table 3.1. These issues need to be revisited and discussed with technical stakeholders to assess which platforms can provide the greatest reach of quality interventions.

The research highlighted that there were too many intervention-area components in the original operational plan (OP) for NNS to address effectively within the required time span. At the beginning of the program, NNS might have been more successful at ensuring effective service delivery with a more careful focus on a limited number of intervention areas, such as infant and young child feeding (IYCF), micronutrients, severe acute malnutrition (SAM)/community-based management of acute malnutrition (CMAM), and nutrition during antenatal care (ANC)/pregnancy. The results from this operational research

Table 3.1   Analyzing Potential of Existing Service Delivery Platforms to Support Reach of Direct Nutrition Intervention in Bangladesh

		Current service delivery platforms	*Analysis*
Domain 1: IYCF and hygiene			
Early initiation of breast-feeding Exclusive breastfeeding for 6 months Age-appropriate complementary feeding for 6–23-month-olds Handwashing with soap at critical times	Age- and practice-specific behavior change counselling, supported by mass media and social mobilization	IMCI+Nutrition and community clinics (both are primarily curative) Limited outreach by HAs, FWVs.	Current investment is mainly in curative. Full reach requires preventive outreach platform that reaches all children in the age group, possibly including NGO platforms.
Domain 2: Micronutrient supplementation			
Vitamin A supplementation	Vitamin A supplementation, biannual	Campaigns for child supplementation Routine supplementation for mothers of newborns	Current strategy is adequate.
IFA supplementation for pregnant women	Iron-folic acid (IFA) tablets during pregnancy and during lactation	ANC for pregnant women *Not clear what platform for lactating women*	Public health system provides ANC to only small proportion of women. Choice of platform needs more analysis.
IFA for adolescent girls	IFA tablets	*Not clear what platform for lactating women and adolescent*	No data to estimate reach. An outreach-based approach may be needed.
Multiple micronutrient powder supplementation for 6–23-month-olds	Counselling about use of multiple micronutrient powders (MNP) and distribution/sales of MNP	Platforms not known but available in diverse ways, such as market, free	Careful gathering of data and analysis needed to identify highest potential platforms.
ORS with zinc to manage diarrhea	Counselling about use of ORS-zinc and distribution/sales of ORS-zinc	IMCI platform for prescription, market purchase of ORS-zinc	ORS reach is already high. Zinc reach needs additional attention.
Domain 3: Consumption of nutrient-rich, fortified foods			
Consumption of iron- and Vitamin-A-rich foods	Several potential interventions, including enhanced agriculture, fortified foods	Primarily market-based platform	Constraints to consumption of these foods requires additional analysis.
Consumption of iodized salt and Vitamin-A-fortified oil		Primarily market-based platform	Additional work is necessary because use is not very high.
Domain 4: Management of acute malnutrition			
Screening and referral of children 0–59 months	Screening at all sick child and well-child care visits	IMCI+Nutrition platform is	Platform reach is limited to those using public health facilities. However, much sick child care happens in private clinics and through informal providers.

table continues next page

Table 3.1 Analyzing Potential of Existing Service Delivery Platforms to Support Reach of DNIs in Bangladesh *(continued)*

		Current service delivery platforms	Analysis
Treatment according to national protocols	Facility- and community-based management strategies needed	SAM treatment centers	No current estimates of unmet need for care. CMAM platforms also need further exploration.
Adequate food and rest during pregnancy and lactation	Counselling of pregnant women and families	ANC for pregnant women	Public health system ANC reach is very limited. More attention is needed to decide on platforms that will deliver full reach of nutrition interventions regardless of ANC provider.
Micronutrient supplementation in pregnancy and lactation	Not clear which micronutrients. Calcium is included in package	ANC for pregnant women	

Source: UNICEF 2014.
Note: ANC = antenatal care; CMAM = community-based management of acute malnutrition; DNI = direct nutrition intervention; FWV = family welfare volunteer; HA = health assistant; IMCI = Integrated Management of Childhood Illnesses; NGO = nongovernmental organization; ORS = oral rehydration solution; SAM = severe acute malnutrition.

underscore issues of capacity and workload of the health care providers at different tiers of the health system. The design elements of delivering additional work for NNS using the existing health system require an approach that ensures that the main goals of NNS are achieved without unduly disrupting regular planned activities of the staff.

Recommendations
- An expert committee, potentially a Steering Committee for Nutrition Implementation, first should prioritize and choose a few key services to deliver as part of NNS. Second, this committee should test the feasibility of these few chosen services with the different Directorate General of Health Services (DGHS) delivery platforms in terms of practicality of delivery and potential for population coverage and impact.
- NNS redevelop very specific implementation plans that map DNIs to specific delivery platforms and help identify the platforms that are best able to reach maximum coverage for specific DNIs.
- Ministry of Health and Family Welfare (MoHFW) explicitly explores the use of other platforms, including nongovernmental organizations (NGO) platforms, to extend reach and achieve greater coverage. For example, several NGOs in Bangladesh have community-level health care providers that can supplement or support health system workers to provide nutrition-focused outreach services.

Institutional Issues and Governance

The research team's results indicate that the maintenance of strong and stable leadership of NNS is an essential element to ensure integrated and well-coordinated comprehensive service delivery by the service. Under the current arrangement, the line director of NNS is also the Director of Institute for Public Health and Nutrition (IPHN). This arrangement apparently is unable to foster effective implementation and coordination of NNS because of recruitment and retention challenges for the Directorship of IPHN.

A second difficulty is the inability of NNS line director to ensure effective coordination with other line directors because the NNS line director is on the same grade level as the other line directors. A careful examination and discussion within the government and among stakeholders to identify a leadership solution for NNS coordination is crucial to NNS success. *The team sees effective leadership as the most fundamental and serious challenge for a cross-sectoral initiative such as NNS.*

Additional significant capacity- and workload-related challenges within NNS/IPHN hamper effective implementation of NNS. Other areas of concern identified were NNS capacity challenges to develop feasible and specific implementation plans to deliver interventions, to develop careful training approaches that work, to maintain and manage records on the training roll-out, and to manage budgets as large as that for NNS. Strengthening capacity in some or all four of these areas also would help ensure that NNS managers could devote more time to managing the program and less time on other tasks, such as negotiating with bureaucracy and attending meetings. Also clear was that that much could be gained by both managers and frontline workers if NNS managers (program managers [PMs] and deputy program managers [DPMs]) took more time to visit frontline service delivery workers in the field.

Development partners certainly could support some of these capacity challenges. However, it is not clear that there is currently a comprehensive, relevant mapping of development partner support to NNS or that NNS is managing development partners and technical institutions to comprehensively address needs in various technical areas, or specific needs in geographic areas.

Recommendations

- Elevate all nutrition/NNS coordination activities to a more senior level within the DGHS leadership (possibly chaired by the DG) to ensure effective coordination.
- Draw on development partners and technical institutes/actors in a careful and strategic manner for specific planning, capacity building, and technical support activities. A comprehensive document that maps the roles of the various development partners is essential to properly utilize available support.
- Establish clear tasks of key development partners and funders for support to NNS.

Training and Roll-Out

The operational assessment and interviews at the national level indicate that NNS training is getting underway after delays in the first year. However, the inadequate record keeping of the training makes it difficult to assess exactly which types of training and support activities were completed in each upazila and how many people at which level were trained. Ensuring excellent record keeping and consolidation around training likely could also address some of the training audit issues raised by interviewees.

From a training design perspective, materials that were reviewed by the research team indicated dense training manuals with limited instructions for facilitators. These materials and the linked training package often required more time to get through than was allocated for the training. If, as recommended by this assessment, the NNS intervention package were streamlined and prioritized, the training manuals could be revised accordingly. The training manuals are being revised. However, to the research team's knowledge, there is no documented structured identification of nutritional capacity gaps and assessment of training needs and effectiveness. Assessment is an area in which technical partners could support NNS. Several high-quality development partner training experiences exist in Bangladesh. Thus, supporting training quality and implementation is a key area in which development partners could support NNS.

Another training challenge is that a large number of frontline health staff receive training from a variety of programs, making the identification and branding of NNS training quite difficult. Monitoring sources of training and the extent of training of workers are, therefore, very challenging, but important—to ensure efficiencies in training on similar topics for health professionals in an integrated health system.

Last, there are several ongoing problems with logistics and supplies for nutrition-related services. For example, upazila staff received nutrition training but did not receive NNS supplies. In addition, reportedly, there has been been a substantial lag between submission of requests for supplies and receiving the latter. NNS has initiated procurement logistics through the Central Medical Stores Depot. Continued work by NNS is necessary to streamline the procurement process with this depot.

Recommendations

- In the immediate short term, NNS must ensure excellent and transparent (ideally, web-based) record keeping, external monitoring, and consolidation of information on training activities. In particular, web-based record keeping could help address some of the training audit issues raised by interviewees.
- *NNS* must draw on development partners and strong implementation organizations to develop a very detailed implementation roll-out plan that is feasible and in line with the goals for coverage and impact.
- In partnership with strong technical partners, *MoHFW* should invest in establishing a high-quality training unit.

Program Implementation/Service Delivery

Service delivery under NNS is intended to occur through diverse delivery platforms: IMCI+Nutrition Corners, ANC, inpatient care, sick-child visits at community clinics, and outreach through health assistants (HAs) and family welfare volunteers (FWVs). Each of these delivery platforms has its inherent challenges related to coverage, reach, quality, and utilization, as well as platform-specific challenges to integrate nutrition interventions, In turn, NNS interventions delivered through these platforms also are subject to platform-specific basic challenges and nutrition integration challenges.

- *IMCI+Nutrition Corners.* Integrated Management of Childhood Illnesses (IMCI) protocols already include guidance on specific nutrition-related activities (such as checking on feeding and assessing weights). However, the nutrition component is lagging behind the basic clinical diagnostic and prescriptive nature of sick-child care. Emphasizing the nutrition activities as part of ongoing IMCI training can strengthen the nutrition component. However, since children coming into IMCI+Nutrition Corners are primarily sick children, targeting IYCF counselling at a very short appointment[1] is particularly challenging (wrong age group, sick children only).
- *ANC.* ANC protocols already include some nutrition focus, and providers do include several nutrition-specific actions in the ANC care provision. The ANC platform is fundamentally prevention focused and directly reaches the target of the nutrition interventions: pregnant women—but only those seeking these antenatal care services, estimated to be less than 30 percent of all pregnant women.
- *Referral and inpatient care for SAM.* Referrals for SAM are limited or inaccurate because providers are not investing in weighing and measurement of children coming into the IMCI+Nutrition Corners. In most facilities observed, the usual number of SAM children managed in the previous month was two or less.
- *Sick-child visits at* community clinics. We observed extremely poor performance related to weighing of sick children seen in the community clinics, in spite of a greater availability of equipment than in IMCI+Nutrition corners. Strengthening care protocols for sick children brought into the community clinics also could strengthen the nutrition-focused service components.
- *Outreach through HAs/FWVs.* The research team did not examine service delivery by HAs and FWVs. Qualitative interviews with these frontline staff revealed their almost complete lack of awareness or knowledge about nutrition-related services and low exposure to NNS training. A detailed assessment of training processes that relate to these frontline workers is essential, as is an assessment of their specific roles within NNS.

Overall, there is great variability in the integration of nutrition interventions and actions into these delivery platforms, and much remains to be done to truly integrate nutrition into these health services. Nevertheless, there are areas of better performance, for example, with IMCI+Nutrition and ANC, but deep challenges relating to service delivery and supervision exist for the community clinics and the outreach services by the HAs and FWAs. Training coverage among these service providers also is low. The research team had no knowledge of any piloting of specific NNS interventions within each of these platforms before implementing mainstreamed services at larger scale, there also is no ongoing learning or review process in place to assess implementation challenges. Therefore, there remains limited scope for learning approaches through the process of implementing NNS via such diverse implementation modalities. The research team's key recommendation is that NNS consider integrating feasibility assessments, technical review missions, and other learning approaches for assessing the delivery of at least a few prioritized critical interventions and identify ways to close potential bottlenecks in program service delivery. Appropriate piloting would have revealed these problems regarding workload and choice of platforms. A continuous learning process, engaging technical partners, can help to strengthen overall implementation plans and provide NNS managers with the opportunity to learn more about on-the-ground implementation processes and to ensure program fidelity and quality with greater confidence.

Recommendations

- NNS should consider integrating feasibility assessments, technical review missions, and other learning approaches for assessing the delivery of at least a few prioritized critical interventions.
- NNS could explore the use of the community groups and community support groups attached to each community clinic in raising awareness of, and demand for, better nutrition-related services.
- MoHFW should rethink moving away from IMCI+Nutrition corners as a central delivery platform for NNS and invest more deeply in an alternative and predominantly outreach-based platform for delivering core preventive NNS to households and children, for example, well-child clinics at all existing health facilities at upazila levels and below, while still ensuring that overall IMCI service delivery remains a focus for sick-child care.
- MoHFW should reexamine and clarify the role of HAs and FWAs, building capacity and monitoring/incentivization for them to deliver preventive nutrition services.

Monitoring and Evaluation

The research team's overall findings on monitoring to strengthen NNS performance is that there are several challenges that could prove to be substantial roadblocks to ensuring that the program performance is on track.

First, record keeping for monitoring purposes appears weak within NNS system. Information on implementation roll-out and development partner support to geographic and technical areas was hard to get or unavailable. Strengthening of record keeping within NNS should be an area to focus on at this stage of the program implementation. This is crucial to ensure that information on implementation roll-out, and development partner support to geographic and technical areas is easily available to all key stakeholders and is routinely updated.

Second, in spite of the development of a set of nutrition indicators for mainstreaming into the health management information system, there are challenges with some indicators (which are close to impossible to assess in a facility-based HMIS). In addition, there is a legitimate concern about overloading frontline workers with excessive record keeping. We recommend a careful review of the current set of NNS indicators for inclusion in the HMIS and prioritization of a few indicators that are indicative of extent and quality of service delivery in the first instance, rather than of actual nutrition statistics such as low birth weight, early initiation of breast feeding, or stunting.

Third, a system for technical monitoring of service quality by experts is largely absent. NNS staff at the Dhaka level are too busy and do not make the needed field visits to examine program performance. Even though some supervisory visits are taking place at the level of the health facilities, it is not clear to the research team whether those visits aim to ascertain both basic service provision and nutrition intervention quality. This is an area where NNS can draw upon the capacity of development partners who have both technical capacity and, in several cases, local field presence. Developing a streamlined technical visit and a web-based data input system for recording site visits might help facilitate organized and systematic field supervision visits.

Recommendations

- Strengthening its own record keeping and reporting is a key focus area for NNS at this stage of program implementation.
- MoHFW needs to (1) make a careful review of the current set of NNS indicators for inclusion in the RHMIS and (2) prioritize a few indicators that are indicative of extent and quality of service delivery, rather than of actual nutrition outcomes such as low birth weight or stunting.
- A system for technical monitoring of service quality by internal and external experts is a critical need. NNS should draw on the capacity of development partners to (1) help develop a streamlined quality assurance system, possibly including a web-based data input system for recording site visits, and (2) help facilitate organized and systematic field supervision visits.

Final Conclusions

This assessment of the current state of NNS is drawn from multiple-data sources. This assessment is meant predominantly to inform revisions to NNS approach and to refocus and identify critical areas for continued investment and support. Although this assessment has identified several substantial challenges, we conclude that the overall NNS effort is an ambitious but valuable approach to examining how best to support nutrition actions through an existing health system with diverse platforms. Focusing on some of the critical challenges related to leadership and coordination in the first instance and on embedding a small core set of interventions into well-matched (for scale, target populations, and potential for impact) health system delivery platforms is most likely to help achieve scale and impact. Strategic investments in ensuring transparency, engaging available technical partners for monitoring and implementation support, and not shying away from other potential high coverage outreach platforms like some NGO platforms also could prove fruitful. Although the Government of Bangladesh, and the health system in particular, must lead the effort to deliver for nutrition, it is clear that development partners who have expressed a commitment to nutrition must coordinate their own activities and provide the support that can deliver on nutrition's potential for Bangladesh.

Note

1. The quantitative observation data indicate that the average time each health care provider spends with each patient is approximately 3.5 minutes.

Qualitative Research and Service Delivery Data

Table A.1 Subnational Interviewees for In-Depth Interviews, by District

Interviewee	Nilphamari	Cox's Bazar	Khulna	Moulavibazar	Total
Medical officers	2	2	2	2	8
Subassistant community medical officers	2	2	2	4	10
Nurses	2	2	2	1	7
Health inspectors	2	2	2	2	8
Assistant health inspectors	2	2	2	1	7
Health assistants	2	2	3	2	9
Family welfare volunteers	2	2	2	2	8
Family welfare assistants	1	2	1	2	6
Family planning assistants	0	0	0	1	1
Assistant family welfare officers	0	0	0	1	1
Community health care providers	2	2	2	2	8
Upazila health and family planning officers	2	2	2	1	7
Residential medical officers	0	0	0	1	1
Upazila family planning officers	2	2	2	2	8
Civil surgeons/district superintendents	1	1	1	1	4
Total	22	23	23	25	93

Table A.2 Types of Data Collection Instruments and Sources of Data Collection for the Survey

Data collection instrument	Sources of data collection
Exit Interview	Caregiver of the children
Under-5 Illness Management Observation Checklist	Observation of case management
ANC Observation Checklist	Observation of case management
Health Care Provider Survey	Health care providers
Facility Assessment Checklist	Person in charge of the facility (civil surgeon, UHFPO, others) and persons designated by him or her

Note: ANC = antenatal care; UHFPO = upazila health and family planning officer.

Table A.3 Frequency of Issues Discussed as Important in Subnational-Level Interviews with Health Officials at Upazila, Union, and Community Levels

Issue raised by interviewee as important	Official post of interviewee									
	HI N = 8	AHI N = 7	Nurse N = 7	SACMO N = 10	HA N = 9	FWA N = 6	FWV N = 8	AFWO N = 1	FPA N = 1	CHCP N = 8
Management and support services										
Is there a problem with retention of medical officers?	Yes: 6	Yes: 5	Yes: 1 / Yes: 1	Yes: 1	Yes: 9	Yes: 6	Yes: 4		Yes: 1	Yes: 8
Is there a problem due to demand for curative services?	Yes: 5	Yes: 6 / No: 1	Yes: 7	Yes: 9	Yes: 9 / No: 1	Yes: 4	Yes: 3 / No: 2	No: 1	Yes: 1	Yes: 6
Training and capacity development										
Had received nutrition training through NNS?	Yes: 4 / No: 3	Yes: 5 / No: 2	No: 7	No: 9	Yes: 6 / No: 1	Yes: 3 / No: 3	No: 6	No: 1	Yes: 1	Yes: 6 / No: 2
Had received ToT through NNS?	No: 3	No: 4		No: 5	No: 5	No: 1	No: 1			N1
Is there a lack of follow-up supervision after training?	Yes: 1 / No: 1	Yes:2	Yes: 1 / No: 2		Yes: 1	Yes: 1 / No: 2			Yes: 1	Yes: 1 / No: 2
Delivery of nutrition services										
Is there a lack of clarity about NNS (apart from BCC)?	Yes: 7	Yes: 3 / No: 1	Yes: 4	Yes: 4 / No: 2	Yes: 4 / No: 2	Yes: 4 / No: 1	Yes: 4 / No: 2	Yes: 1	N0: 1	Yes: 6 / No: 1
Are preventive services being crowded out due to demand for curative services?	Yes: 2	Yes: 1	Yes: 3 / No: 1	Yes: 3 / No: 1	Yes: 3 / No: 1		Yes:1 / No: 1		Yes: 1	Yes: 4
Is there a lack of medicine or supplement supply?	Yes: 2 / No: 3	Yes: 1 / No: 4	Yes: 4 / No: 2	Yes: 3 / No: 4	Yes: 3 / No: 5	No: 3	Yes: 3 / No: 1	No: 1	Yes: 1	Yes: 2 / No: 4
Is treatment of malnutrition (SAM or MAM) inadequate?	Yes: 1 / No: 1	N 4	Yes: 2 / No: 3	Yes: 1 / No: 4	Yes: 1 / No: 4	Yes: 2 / No: 1	No: 2	Yes: 1	Yes: 1	Yes: 3 / No: 1
Monitoring and evaluation										
Is there a lack of clarity on monitoring requirements?	Yes: 2	Yes: 5	Yes: 3	Yes: 5 / No: 1	Yes: 5	Yes: 5	Yes: 2	Yes: 1	Yes: 1	Yes: 3
Is there a lack of M&E tools?		Yes: 2 / No: 2							Yes: 1	
Any M&E conducted for nutrition inputs?			No: 2		Yes: 2	Yes: 2	No: 1		Yes: 1	No: 1
Exposure to interventions										
Has coverage improved after the establishment of CCs?	Yes: 5	Yes: 6		Yes: 2	Yes: 9	Yes: 4	Yes: 1	Yes: 1	Yes: 1	Yes: 8
Are UHCs prevented from providing adequate nutrition services due to poor staffing?	Yes: 4 / No: 1	Yes: 5 / No: 1	Yes: 3	Yes: 9		Yes: 2				

HI = health inspector; AHI = assistant health inspector; SACMO = subassistant community medical officer; HA = health assistant; FWA = family welfare assistant; FWV = family welfare volunteer; AFWO = assistant family welfare officer; FPA = family planning assistant; CHCP = community health care provider.

Table A.4 Characteristics of Children, Caregivers, and Types of Health Care Providers Observed during Case Management at IMCI Nutrition Corners

Characteristics	n	Percent
Age of child (months)		
0–11	214	26.2
12–23	179	21.9
24–35	149	18.2
36–47	141	17.2
48–60	133	16.3
Sex of child		
Male	442	54.1
Female	374	45.8
Caregiver		
Biological parent	707	86.6
Others	109	13.3

Note: There were a total of 816 children. IMCI = Integrated Management of Childhood Illnesses.

Table A.5 Number of Upazila That Received Training, 2012–14

Type of training	2012	2013	2014	Total
Only basic nutrition	20	23	9	52
Only logistics	—	49	—	49
Basic nutrition + logistics	—	—	—	43

Note: — = not available.

Table A.6 Availability of Trained Health Care Providers for ANC/PNC Services at Different Levels of Health Facilities

Service level	Type of training	Medical officer	Nurse	Subassistant community medical officer	Family welfare volunteer	Community health care provide	Health assistant
District hospital	Total	10	10	0	0	0	0
	NNS trained	0	1	—	—	—	—
	IYCF trained	2	4	—	—	—	—
Upazila hospital	Total	11	7	8	2	0	0
	NNS trained	7	2	0	0	—	—
	IYCF trained	3	1	0	1	—	—
Upazila health and family welfare centre	Total	0	0	12	10	1	0
	NNS trained	—	—	1	0	1	—
	IYCF trained	—	—	1	1	0	—
Community clinic	Total	0	0	1	—	11	4
	NNS trained	—	—	0	—	3	2
	IYCF trained	—	—	0	—	1	—

Notes: ANC = antenatal care; IYCF = infant and young child feeding; NNS = National Nutrition Service; PNC = postnatal care.
— = not available.

Bangladesh National Nutrition Services • http://dx.doi.org/10.1596/978-1-4648-0640-7

Table A.7   Availability of Trained Health Care Providers for Illness Management of Children Younger Than Five Years of Age at Different Levels of Health Facilities

Service level	Type of training	Medical officer	Nurse	Subassistant community medical officer	Family welfare volunteer	Community health care provide	Health assistant
District hospital	Total	9	12	2	0	0	0
	NNS trained	2	6	0	—	—	—
	IYCF trained	3	6	0	—	—	—
Upazila hospital	Total	9	5	21	0	0	0
	NNS trained	2	3	2	—	—	—
	IYCF trained	3	0	1	—	—	—
Upazila health and family welfare centre	Total	0	0	10	9	1	0
	NNS trained	—	—	4	1	1	—
	IYCF trained	—	—	1	1	—	—
Community clinic	Total	0	0	1	0	9	2
	NNS trained	—	—	0	—	4	1
	IYCF trained	—	—	0	—	5	1

Notes: ANC = antenatal care; IYCF = infant and young child feeding; NNS = National Nutrition Service; PNC = postnatal care.— = not available.

Table A.8   Availability of Functioning Equipment, Logistics, and Job Aides at Different Service Delivery Platforms of Survey Health Facilities at District, Upazila, and Union Levels

Equipment, logistics, and job aides	Number of facilities with functioning equipment
ANC/PNC	
Adult weighing scale	41
Height scale	23
Blood pressure machine	35
Stethoscope	40
Measuring tape	19
Thermometer	25
Record-keeping register	33
Pictorial cards with maternal danger signs	25
Guideline on iron-folic acid /anemia prevention and control	11
Guideline on distribution of Vitamin A	9
Basic Nutrition Training Guideline (inside ANC/PNC room)	7
Infant and young child feeding manual	6
Inpatient	
Severe acute malnutrition management protocol/guideline	5
Acute malnutrition management protocol/guideline	4
Thermometer	15
Measuring cup/spoon	8
Nasogastric tubes	8
Needles and syringes	13
Butterfly needle of different size	13
Weighing machine	14

Notes: ANC = antenatal care; PNC = postnatal care.

Table A.9 Reasons for Visiting the Facility, Reported by Caregivers at Exit Interviews

Reasons for visiting the facility	Number of children with problem (N = 816)	Percent
Diarrhea	143[a]	17.5
Vomiting	46	5.7
Fever/malaria	312	38.2
Fast/difficult breathing/cough/pneumonia	217	26.6
Ear problem	19	2.3
Well-child visit	1	0.1
Others	415	50.9

a. Total number of children with a problem is greater than 816 because multiple problems were reported by some children. For the same reason, percentages exceed 100.

Table A.10 Intended Recipients of Training of Trainers and Recipients of Cascade Training, by Training Type

	Training Type			
	SAM	CMAM	IYCF	Basic Nutrition Training
Recipients of training of trainers				
Junior consultant—pediatrics/medical officer		×		
Medical officer/registrar/assistant registrar	×			
Medical officer–civil surgeon				
Medical officer–district superintendent				
Medical officer–maternal and child health			×	×
Medical officer–poverty, health, and nutrition			×	×
Pediatrics consultant/assistant professor	×	×		
Upazila health and family planning officer		×	×	×
Recipients of cascade training				
Assistant health inspector		×	×	×
Community health care provider		×	×	×
Family planning inspector		×	×	×
Family welfare assistant		×	×	×
Family welfare volunteer		×	×	×
Health assistant		×	×	×
Health inspector		×	×	×
Medical officer		×	×	
Medical officer–civil surgeon	×			
Medical officer–district superintendent	×			
Medical officer–maternal and child health	×			
Medical officer–poverty, health, and nutrition	×			
Pediatrics consultant	×			

table continues next page

Bangladesh National Nutrition Services • http://dx.doi.org/10.1596/978-1-4648-0640-7

Table A.10 Intended Recipients of Training of Trainers and Recipients of Cascade Training, by Training Type *(continued)*

| | *Training Type* | | | |
	SAM	*CMAM*	*IYCF*	*Basic Nutrition Training*
Senior staff nurse	×	×	×	
SI				×
Subassistant community medical officer		×	×	
Upazila family planning officer		×	×	
Upazila family welfare volunteer/senior family welfare volunteer		×	×	

Notes: CMAM = community-based management of acute malnutrition; IYCF = infant and young child feeding; SAM = severe acute malnutrition.

Community Clinics Data

Table B.1 Number of Health Care Providers with Basic Nutrition Training in Community Clinics

	CHCP (N = 14)	FWA (N = 5)	Total (N = 19)
Received Basic Nutrition Training by NNS			
Yes	6	1	7
No	8	4	12

Note: CHCP = community health care provider; FWA = family welfare assistant; NNS = National Nutrition Service.

Table B.2 Number of Health Facilities with Functioning Height and Weight Machine

	District hospitals (N = 6)	Upazila health complex (N = 12)	Upazila health and family welfare centre (N = 14)	Community clinic (N = 12)	Total (N = 44)
Does the facility have functioning height and weight scale?					
Yes	3	5	4	11	23
No	3	7	10	1	21

Table B.3 Observation of Illness Management of Children Younger Than Five Years of Age at Community Clinics (N = 66)

	Child checked for three danger signs	Measure and record weight of the child	Measure and record height of the child
Did the health worker provide the following services?			
Yes	2	3	1
No	64	63	65

Table B.4   Satisfaction with Services at Community Clinics as Reported by the Caregivers (*N* = 65)

	Very bad	Bad	Average	Good	Very Good
How is the transportation system from your house to this center?	1	8	15	38	3
How is the situation of the area in which you wait for the doctor?	0	1	27	35	2
How is the advice/prescription of the doctor?	0	0	22	40	3

Table B.5   Number of Times Different Health Facilities Were Visited by an External Supervisor in the Past Six Months

	Were not visited	Visited 1–3 times	Visited 4–6 times	Visited more than 6 times	Total
District hospital	1	0	4	1	6
Upazila health complex	4	2	2	4	12
Upazila health and family welfare centre	4	5	2	3	14
Community clinic	3	4	3	2	12

APPENDIX C

Training Data

Table C.1   Number of Recipients (ToT or Cascade) until December 2013, by Training Type

Training type	ToT recipients	Number of health workers trained until December 2013	Cascade training recipients	Number of health care providers trained until December 2013
SAM	Pediatrics consultant/assistant professor	45	Pediatrics consultant	170
			MOPHN	482
			MOMCH	0
	Medical officer/registrar/assistant registrar	77	MODC/MOCS	0
			SSN	322
CMAM	Pediatrics consultant/assistant professor	83	MO	0
			UFPO	0
			SACMO	0
			SSN	0
	UHFPO, MOPHN, MOMCH	90	FWV	0
			UFWV/senior FWV	0
			HA	0
			CHCP	0
			FWA	0
			HI	0
			AHI	0
IYCF	UHFPO	203	MO	304
			UFPO	38
	MOPHN	251	SACMO	304
			Nursing supervisor/ SSN/SN	409
		0	FWV	319
	MOMCH		UFWV/senior FWV	0
			HA	2161
	OBGYN/pediatrics consultant	0	CHCP	1051
			FWA	1884

table continues next page

Table C.1 Number of Recipients (ToT or Cascade) until December 2013, by Training Type *(continued)*

Training type	ToT recipients	Number of health workers trained until December 2013	Cascade training recipients	Number of health care providers trained until December 2013
	SSN	0	MT (EPI)	38
			HI	114
			AHI	261
			FPI	118
Basic Nutrition Training	UHFPO	130	SACMO	2010
	UFPO	130	HA	4762
	MOPHN	130	FWA	6100
	MOMCH	130	CHCP	3518
	MODC	0	FWV	1222

Source: GoB 2014b.

Figure C.2 Number of Upazila Receiving Different Nutrition Trainings for the First Time, 2012–14

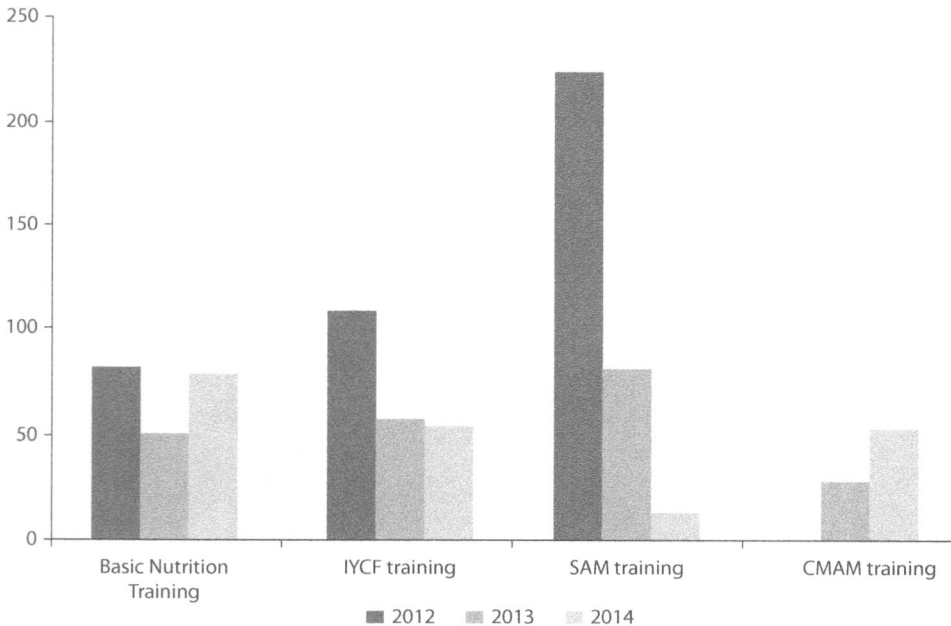

Notes: CMAM = community-based management of acute malnutrition; IYCF = infant and young child feeding; SAM = severe acute malnutrition.
Source: GoB 2014b.

References

GoB (Government of the People's Republic of Bangladesh). 2011a. "Health, Population and Nutrition Sector Development Program (2011–2016) PIP (Program Implementation Plan), Vol. I. Planning Wing 3." Ministry of Health and Family Welfare, GoB, Dhaka.

_____. 2011b. "National Nutrition Services (NNS) Jatiya Pushti Seba: A Mainstreamed and Integrated Approach for Addressing Malnutrition." Institute for Public Health and Nutrition, Ministry of Public Health, GoB, Dhaka.

_____. 2011c. "Operational Plan for National Nutrition Services, July 2011–June 2016." Health, Population and Nutrition Sector Development Program, Director General of Health Services Ministry of Health and Family Welfare, GoB, Dhaka.

_____. 2013a. "Basic Nutrition Training Manual for Field Level Service Provider." IPHN and MoHFW, GoB, Dhaka.

_____. 2013b. "Comprehensive Training Plan for National Nutrition Services." IPHN (Institute for Public Health and Nutrition, GoB, Dhaka. November.

_____. 2014a. "Strategic Plan for Health, Population and Nutrition Sector Development Program (HPNSDP)." Ministry of Health and Family Welfare, GoB, Dhaka.

_____. 2014b. Working Paper on NNS Implementation in First 18 Months. Institute for Public Health and Nutrition, GoB, Dhaka.

GoB (Government of the People's Republic of Bangladesh) and World Bank. "The Modalities for the Implementation of the National Nutrition Services."

Mbuya, N. K. 2011. "The National Nutrition Program (NNP) Survey, 2010: An Assessment of Area-Based Community Nutrition (ABCN) Services in Bangladesh." Unpublished Report, World Bank, Washington, DC.

UNICEF (United Nations Children's Fund) Bangladesh. 2014. "Mid-Term Review Report, Maternal and Child Nutrition Programme, Government of Bangladesh. UNICEF Country Programme (2012–16)." UNICEF Bangladesh, Dhaka. June.

World Bank. 2011. "The National Nutrition Program (NNP) Survey, 2010: An Assessment of Area-Based Community Nutrition (ABCN) Services in Bangladesh." Unpublished World Bank, Washington, DC.

Environmental Benefits Statement

The World Bank Group is committed to reducing its environmental footprint. In support of this commitment, the Publishing and Knowledge Division leverages electronic publishing options and print-on-demand technology, which is located in regional hubs worldwide. Together, these initiatives enable print runs to be lowered and shipping distances decreased, resulting in reduced paper consumption, chemical use, greenhouse gas emissions, and waste.

The Publishing and Knowledge Division follows the recommended standards for paper use set by the Green Press Initiative. The majority of our books are printed on Forest Stewardship Council (FSC)–certified paper, with nearly all containing 50–100 percent recycled content. The recycled fiber in our book paper is either unbleached or bleached using totally chlorine free (TCF), processed chlorine free (PCF), or enhanced elemental chlorine free (EECF) processes.

More information about the Bank's environmental philosophy can be found at http://crinfo.worldbank.org/wbcrinfo/node/4.

green
press
INITIATIVE

www.ingramcontent.com/pod-product-compliance
Lightning Source LLC
Chambersburg PA
CBHW080000280326
41935CB00013B/1706